SHE WON THE RACE

FOOTPRINTS OF CANCER

SHE WON THE RACE

A TRUE STORY

MARTHA AXMANN

Pleasant Word (a division of WinePress Publishing, PO Box 428, Enumclaw, WA 98022) functions only as book publisher. As such, the ultimate design, content, editorial accuracy, and views expressed or implied in this work are those of the author.

Unless otherwise noted, all Scriptures are taken from the *Holy Bible, New International Version*®, *NIV*®. Copyright © 1973, 1978, 1984 by the International Bible Society. Used by permission of Zondervan. All rights reserved.

Scripture references marked NKJV are taken from the *New King James Version*. Copyright ©1982 by Thomas Nelson, Inc. Used by permission. All rights reserved.

Scripture references marked KJV are taken from the *King James Version* of the Bible.

ISBN 13: 978-1-4141-1249-7
ISBN 10: 1-4141-1249-1
Library of Congress Catalog Card Number: 2008904637

CONTENTS

FOREWORD

MARTHA AXMANN HAS opened the windows of her soul in this book, sharing with us the story of Robyn. More deeply, she has shared her own story as a wife and mother who has loved and exulted in the life of a beautiful, precious daughter who committed herself to a bold calling to give herself for others. Martha Axmann begins by telling the story of her own growing up and coming of age in the American South, falling in love and living what seems to be the perfect American family dream. She had a loving, supportive husband and a son and a daughter. All were faithful to church and loving of others. In retrospect, her life seemed so right, so much what she wanted for her own daughter, now the age Martha Axmann had been when she had begun her own young family.

Why does Martha have to suffer the worst possible loss—the loss of a child? No parent ever imagines burying their own child, particularly a child in the first bloom of adulthood. And why, still later, the suffering and death of her husband? He, too, slipped from her as she tried to hold on through sheer force of will and prayer, curled in his arms each night, knowing that cancer was taking him away, too.

Where does she find the strength to turn from this second grave of one who was her life and find a way onward?

It is too easy to offer theological truths such as "God does not cause suffering; rather, God suffers with us," or "God never leaves us alone," or "it is a mystery; we see through a glass darkly." Theological truths without story, though, are like the friends of Job, pronouncing to their "friend" what they believed to be the meaning of suffering. Instead of theological truths, God offers us a story—a story of sending his only son to show us how to live by example, only to watch him live too short a life, then suffer and die a painful, protracted death. We can find God in this story more than we can in a set of so-called "truths." In the same way, we walk with one another with the greatest comfort and meaning when we share our own stories with one another.

It is in that spirit that Martha Axmann has so transparently shared her life with us. If you are standing helplessly by while your friend, like Job, sits in a heap of ashes and grief, the story of how ever-widening communities of faith were present in meaningful ways for Martha Axmann will show you how to be a truly caring friend.

If you are suffering, you own unspeakable loss; this book's message is that you are not alone. When Mary stood at the foot of the cross watching her son die, with her stood friends. Martha Axmann offers to stand with you as you suffer loss through this story—the story of Robyn.

—**Diana Garland,** PH.D.
Dean, Baylor School of Social Work
Waco, Texas
October 15, 2006

ACKNOWLEDGMENTS

I WANT TO THANK God for allowing me to listen to him and respond to his call in asking me to write this book. All of Robyn's friends have been such an encouragement to me and helped me with memories of Robyn. I also would like to thank the following people who helped me in different ways to bring this book to completion: Sharon Brisken, Sheila Ingle, Dr. Bob Hanley, Edna Ellison, Dr. Diana Garland, Livia Mitchell, and Jackson Bundy. My family and church friends have constantly lifted me in prayers and given me inspiration to finish this task.

To God be the Glory,
Martha Axmann

PROLOGUE

I have fought the good fight, I have finished the race, I have kept the faith. Now there is in store for me the crown of righteousness, which the Lord, the righteous Judge, will award to me on that day.
　　　　　　　　　　　　　　　　　　　　　—2 Timothy 4:7-8

GOD CHOSE FOR my daughter, Robyn, to finish her race on earth on March 11, 1991, at the early age of twenty-six. I had no choice but to give her back to him. I can't see or understand why. However, someday, praise God, I will know. For now I have to exercise faith beyond what I can see and know in my limited human way and bridge this void, this death, and this horror with faith that only God can give me.

A few days following Robyn's entrance into heaven, I wrote this prayer:

Dear God, help me fill this valley of sadness with mountains of divine joy and endless praise and eternal love—the void of her enthusiasm with the harmony of her music, the absence of her presence with the presence of your Spirit, the beauty of her perfect smile with the beauty of a Christian witness, the touch of her caring heart with a life of service to others, the friendship of a best friend with an example of what friends are for, the love of my only daughter with spiritual love that radiates to others.

As I know she's now with you, God, fulfilling a divine task, give us the same determination we saw in her to serve you more completely each day.

Thank you, God, for the privilege of having her for these twenty-six years.

I know all things work together for good for those who love the Lord (Romans 8:28). However, as a mother, I continued to seek answers to help me as I ran from depression. One day I turned on the Focus on the Family radio program, and I felt God speak to me through that day's guest. Steve Saint, author of *The End of the Spear*, told about his daughter, Stephanie, and how her death had, for a time, devastated his walk with God. I just sat there and cried because I felt again the pain of losing a child. Steve Saint's feelings as a father were so much like my feelings as a mother! I felt God nudging me to write about Robyn.

One of the scriptures read at Robyn's graveside was 1 Corinthians 15:58: "Therefore, my dear brothers, stand firm. Let nothing move you. Always give yourselves fully to the work of the Lord, because you know that your labor in the Lord is not in vain."

Thank you, Lord.

I will have to say honestly that my faith was shaken after Robyn was taken—she was so young and had such potential—and then my husband also died, at a time when we could have spent more time together enjoying some of the things he had worked so hard for all his life. However, I will hasten to say, as I pray daily, God is with me, and he has provided for me and protected me. I constantly say, "Lord, tell me what you have for me to do for your glory, and how I may serve you better and more completely."

That's why I am writing this book. I felt God kept saying to me, "Martha, when are you going to do what I want you to do so that it might bless and encourage others through trials in their lives?"

But it was so painful for me to get everything about Robyn back out. I ran from that. I could always think of something else I wanted to do. I tried to do things that would fill my time and also use my talents and serve God. I tutored at my home for a while, I did substitute teaching, I taught in an adult reading program, and I served on the foster care board for Spartanburg County. I also taught in an after-school program for the Boys & Girls Club, helping students pull up their test scores. I served as president of the Sanctuary Choir at my church and served on several committees. I was elected to the board of trustees at Anderson. I enjoyed serving in each of these endeavors.

I was prodded every now and then, *When are you going to finish the writing?* When I was serving on the board at Anderson, one of Robyn's friends became ill with leukemia and died. I wished my story were written down so I could hand it to her parents; it would have been a blessing to them. A young girl from my church was killed in a car accident, and I was reminded again. Robyn's friends sometimes said to me, "You know, you could write about Robyn." Another young girl from Anderson was killed in a car wreck on the way to a ball game with other students. I wrote her parents a note, expressing that I understood what they were going through. This was another reminder.

Then one day when I was serving on a committee at my church, I had to write something up for one of the ministers. After this, just "out of the blue," he said, "Martha, just put a pencil in your hand and it's amazing what you can do."

With God's help, I've tried to put my story into words. I pray this will be a blessing to every soul who reads it and a soul winner for those who don't know God yet. I could not live and keep my mind and go through these experiences without God and knowing someday I will see Robyn and William again.

Steve Saint's testimony on the Focus on the Family radio broadcast spoke to me of this. When Steve was a boy, his father, a missionary in the jungles of South America, had been killed by the people he was trying to serve. One of the warriors, named Mincaye, later became a Christian and a friend to Steve. Steve invited Mincaye to his home in the States. There Mincaye witnessed the sudden and unexpected death of Steve's college-age daughter, Stephanie, due to a cerebral hemorrhage.

In the emergency room, when Mincaye saw Stephanie unconscious, covered with tubes and wires and surrounded by medical workers, he became very frustrated and wanted to know who was doing this. All Steve could say was, "No one is doing this, Mincaye. Steph is real sick. People are trying to help her."

As the flurry of activity around them continued, Mincaye's face was totally changed to a look of peace and confidence. "Don't you see," he asked Steve, "that God is doing this himself? He is taking Steph to live with him in heaven."

Steve slowly realized this had to be part of the story God was writing with their lives. Somehow, beyond his ability to comprehend this terrible trauma, it would eventually and mysteriously prove to be a cornerstone of God's plan for them. Steve bowed his head and prayed, "Change my heart, O God."

Just as Steve Saint prayed for God to change his heart, each day I pray the same. To share Robyn's story was a change for me. Another step in my changing was to *write* Robyn's story. My prayer for you, the reader, is that God will also change your heart and draw you close to himself.

> Change My Heart, Oh God,
> Make it ever new,
> Change my heart, Oh God,
> May I be like you.

PROLOGUE

You are the potter,
I am the clay
Mold me and make me
This is what I pray.

Change My Heart, Oh God.
Make it ever new
Change My Heart, Oh God
May I be like you!

"Poopsie"

It was typical of Robyn to give everyone a nickname. Her jovial personality was evident in all her activities. She concocted a name for me sometime when she was in high school. Somehow I was her "Poopsie." Where she got that from, I'll never know.

CHAPTER 1

BEGINNINGS

I AM THE youngest of five children—four girls and one boy. I was raised in the small town of Cowpens, South Carolina, near Spartanburg. My mom taught school until she had children, and Daddy worked in a small bank until it closed. Then Daddy became a part-time farmer and service station owner, and eventually he went into the used-car business.

Each of my parents had different talents. Daddy, a gifted business-man and a Purple Heart WWI veteran, also knew how to invest and save his earnings. He provided a good home and college educations for his five children. Mom, talented in music and teaching, did a lot of church work and was involved in community activities.

I am thankful to this day for Christian parents and the love, fellowship, and support of a small community and church. More than once since becoming an adult, I've been told I lived a very sheltered life, and compared to today's world, I did. However, as I look back to my roots, I see that parents, church, and community are the glue that holds me together, the foundation of the workings of the inner person I am today.

As we go along in life, we continually seek God's will in major decisions. Sometimes I am shocked or amazed at how I have felt his leading, but at other times I have had to keep seeking a final answer. When I was seeking God's will regarding leaving home and going to college, I felt lost. All my siblings had finished college and held jobs in other places, and for six years it had been just Mom and Daddy and me living together in our small town. In many ways I was not prepared to face everyday trials without this close home environment, and I wasn't too thrilled at the idea of leaving it.

I had always wanted to be a schoolteacher. When I was a small child, I played school with my dolls, my dogs, my friends, Daddy, and anything or anyone else who would sit at the desks I arranged like a schoolroom. I was always the teacher, with chalk in one hand and a ruler in the other. I could keep my dogs sitting in their desks in rows, listening to what I said, and Daddy loved it. He was always the behavior problem—he liked to chew tobacco and spit. Since I had to have school after he got home from work, and this was his time to relax, I had to let him chew. The dogs loved it. Daddy often came up with off-the-wall remarks that were not appropriate for the classroom either—bad influence on the dogs. One day a neighbor said to me that she didn't know if I was going to be a schoolteacher or a veterinarian, but she believed I could do either. I knew I had to go to college to be prepared.

I felt I did not want to go to a large college, but I did not know where I wanted to go. The Lord was leading me at this time, although I did not realize it. One day a lady knocked on our door, and my mom let her in. She said she wanted to talk with me and that she was a field representative from Anderson College in Anderson, South Carolina. At that time, Anderson was a two-year junior college. I liked what she said. After a visit to the campus and the offer of a voice scholarship, I decided I would go to Anderson. After being at Anderson for several months, I knew I was where God wanted me to be.

I took basic courses that would transfer to a four-year college; I knew I had to go on to a four-year college to get my degree. Then after two years came another major decision—where to go next. Anderson had a good relationship with Furman University in Greenville, South Carolina; both of them were Baptist schools. Several of my close friends planned to take the test to see if they could get into Furman, and I decided I would go with them and try also. Difficult, standardized, timed, and long, the test almost defeated me, but I was determined. When I got my letter of acceptance, I was thrilled and called my parents right away. We all felt Furman was where I was to finish my education.

God was leading me all the time.

Not long after I arrived at Furman, a close friend of mine from my Anderson College days told me about a boy who wanted to go out with me. President of his class, everyone on campus knew him. I was not interested at the time because I was going with someone else. This boy kept pursuing me through my friend, however, and finally I agreed to a double date.

I knew right away that William Axmann was smart, competent, and athletic. I continued my other dating relationship, but somehow I felt God telling me that William Axmann was going to be my husband. I could not give in to that nudging of the Holy Spirit, but William persisted, and I finally accepted a going-steady ring from him. He was an outstanding leader and student at Furman, and it was an honor to be known as his girlfriend. From then on we were inseparable.

William did not have a car, but I needed a car to do my student teaching, so Daddy let me have an old Ford from his used-car lot to get back and forth. (We didn't tell Daddy it was badly needed to date with also!) My siblings really gave Dad a hard time for giving me a car, complaining that they never got cars in college, and to this day I still hear this from them! The old Ford was wonderful for my student teaching, however, and William and I liked having a way to get off campus. Prior to this, we dated on campus or double-dated with friends. Occasionally, a close friend lent William his car.

Now, understand, my Ford did not have all the bells and whistles it needed. Daddy let me know, in no uncertain terms, how cautious I was to be, and I had a very limited amount of money for gas. When William and I went out in the Ford, we were careful not to go very far from Furman. The passenger door stuck and made an awful cracking noise when it opened. I was really particular about where I was when I opened that door; everyone jumped and looked to see what had made the loud noise. It was a little embarrassing.

One night, as we came back from town, the lights got dimmer and dimmer. William drove slowly until we got back to campus. There were no lights at all by then. We breathed sighs of relief—at least we didn't get stopped or have an accident—I knew Daddy would not have liked that! Living dangerously as a college kid was challenging.

The army had loaned William the money for his education at Furman and required two years of active duty service in return. After graduation, William went to Texas for a year to fulfill his duty to the army, and I went to Atlanta, Georgia, with two other girls from Furman to teach school there. William came home around Christmastime and gave me a diamond, and we were married in July. We lived in Connecticut, where he was serving his second year in the army.

William had already been in Connecticut for several months before we were married, so he talked to several of the school districts there about a teaching job for me. I interviewed with those closest to the base where he was stationed, and had several opportunities. I signed a contract with a school in Southington, Connecticut, about fifteen miles from where we were stationed. It looked like a good situation. The school was new and I liked the grade level.

When I signed the contract, I was told about another teacher who might like to carpool with me. Mrs. Light lived about five miles from our home. William did not have to worry about getting to work because we lived on the base, and I could have the car to go to school. I called Mrs. Light immediately.

Mrs. Light was much older than I and had been teaching a long time. She also had been married long enough to tell her husband what to do! Mrs. Light and I took turns driving each week. Inside her car she had posted a note requesting passengers not to smoke while riding in her vehicle. I was allergic to cigarette smoke, but I asked her one day why she had that note in her car, and she said it was for her husband. Now, being just married and very much in love, I thought this was very strange. Couldn't she just ask him not to smoke in her car? However, as I got to know her better, I learned her perspective on marriage differed from mine.

Mrs. Light told me, after about a month of riding together, that I should carry a bag in the car packed with my pajamas, toothbrush, and change of clothes—winter was approaching, and we might not be able to drive home every day. Now, this did not sit too well with me because I was newly married. I needed to get home to see William every night! But since I had never lived up north, I did not realize that snow came often, quickly, and in truckloads.

This became a reality one day when it started snowing in the morning while we were at school. In Connecticut, school officials did not call off school right away as is done in the South, where I had lived all my life. I became more and more concerned as I saw the snow begin to cover the road and grounds outside my classroom window. That week we were driving my car, a Chevrolet with no four-wheel drive and with a large rear end that slid around in bad weather.

I was determined to make it home. We got about halfway and came to a huge hill, and I could not make that car go up that hill. Every time I got about halfway up, the car started sliding sideways, wheels spinning. After I tried three times and slid back down each time, a policeman tapped on the window and asked if he could try. He got in and somehow made the grade. I was so thankful! I certainly did not want to spend the night in a cold car with Mrs. Light saying "I told you so." We just poked all the way home; it took us a long time. As dark began to fall, I was so thankful to pull up to my house and see William, and he felt the same way. I needed that special TLC that only William could render.

I was beginning to miss my South Carolina home, parents, friends, and weather. William was better adjusted to being away because of his time in Texas. I didn't even know if we were going to be able to go home for Christmas that year, and I had never been away from home on Christmas. Sometimes William had to work all night or even a long weekend, and I was miserable. To help my loneliness, William decided to get me a dog—a dachshund. The dog was a lot of company and slept right by my side of the bed.

Besides missing my family, I also felt uncomfortable at the school where I taught, which was very different from any school I had attended or had experienced in my student teaching at Furman. I taught a combination first- and second-grade class, which is difficult for a new teacher. Although the school was a public school, most of the teachers and students were Catholic. The students brought an offering to school about twice a week to give to the nuns. All during those days, I heard the sound of money dropping to the floor or the students playing with it at their desks. At the end of the school day, the nuns came to my class and taught my students about their religion. I am a Southern Baptist, so the Catholic emphasis challenged me.

The teachers' lounge provided another difficult situation. All the teachers, both male and female, shared the lounge. We had a male principal and several male teachers, and some of the teachers went to the lounge just to talk. The only adult bathroom was in this lounge. By the time I had a break, I was "bursting at the seams," and I would go barreling down the hall to the lounge, only to find men and women sitting there talking. I felt very uncomfortable even using the bathroom. Needless to say, I learned a lot of bladder control that year.

One day when I came into the lounge, there were more men than women, so I thought I would just wait to use the bathroom until some of the men left. All the chairs in the lounge were taken, but one chair did have wooden arms. As one of the gentlemen offered to get up, I said, "Oh, no. Don't get up. I'll just sit on the handle of this chair." Everyone thought it was hilarious that I said *handle* instead of *arm*. The teachers loved to hear me talk and would ask me to talk for them; my southern drawl was entertaining.

CHAPTER 2

GIFTS FROM HEAVEN

WILLIAM HAD SAID we would go back to South Carolina when his year in Connecticut was over. I was relying on that time frame. We both wanted to start our family, and by the end of the school year I was pregnant.

As we were contemplating going home, William received word that the army wanted him to stay in. He thought he might have to stay because of Vietnam and was offered another promotion if he would stay in, but he wanted to get out because he had really had enough of army life. If he had not received his discharge when he did, he would have been sent to Vietnam. We felt like God was in control, and we were most grateful.

I look back on our time in Connecticut with a bag of good memories and feel like we did some fruitful serving there. William did such a great job in the army as a first lieutenant. He was, in charge of a very important investigation for a problem that arose on the base thorough and meticulous and was put. Through many hours of work, he found out the truth in the situation and the problem was solved. Hopefully, I was able to influence some of the teachers, parents, and students at my school. We wanted to make a difference while we were there.

While we were in Connecticut, we were asked to help start a Southern Baptist church in New Britain along with four other couples. This was a wonderful experience. We met so many people from various walks of life and different religions. We gained a lot of experience trying to witness in a different environment and with limited resources. We met in the YMCA building. Somehow I was assigned to work with the music, and we really had nothing to work with. We didn't even have hymnals. There was one little keyboard that someone had brought in and tried to play. We sang very familiar songs. The people attending the mission were either off the street or interested visitors, so they were not too familiar with the old Southern Baptist hymns. With God's help, we eventually got some hymnals from a church that had bought new books and gave us the old ones, and we had a small choir. Later, a piano was donated and we hauled that across New Britain in a borrowed truck and got it inside the church. By this time we had acquired an old church building that some people had moved out of, and this made everyone feel more like we were worshipping in a real church. We called a pastor and were eventually constituted into a Southern Baptist congregation.

But it was great preparing to go home. We didn't have to bother with a moving van because we didn't have any furniture. We had lived on the army base in a furnished house, so we didn't have much to pack; I had left all our wedding gifts packed up at home.

The doctor first said I might have to fly since I was in early pregnancy, but I did not want to do that. William mapped out a way home, with frequent stops (against his male inclination), since the doctor had advised this. We did some sightseeing along the way. We thoroughly enjoyed the trip, and getting back home to South Carolina was so exciting and good.

Since William did not have a job, he started immediately sending out resumes and going for interviews. Not having a home yet in South Carolina, we divided the time between William's parents' home in Anderson, and my parents' home in Spartanburg. This was not easy, packing and unpacking and adjusting to others' schedules. For several months, we lived out of our suitcases. William's parents had a small two-bedroom home, with only one bathroom, and my parents had a larger house with two bathrooms, although one was on the back porch and not heated.

My dad knew a little about Milliken & Company in Spartanburg, and suggested William send a resume there. William did and went for an interview, and they hired him. He was asked to go to Hartsville, South Carolina, as an industrial engineer. The company moved us down there, and we rented a small two-bedroom house not far from the mill where William would be working. We got everything moved in except the foot of the bed. The movers lost the footboard, and we had only the one bed. We had to buy a bed frame to hold up the bed because they never found it.

It was so good to finally have our own home that I could fix the way I wanted, even though we did not have much furniture. Soon my parents came to Hartsville. Daddy said, "I want you to go and pick out something for your living room." I was so excited and pleased. Now we had three rooms with furniture!

I got under the care of a gynecologist there. We had only one car, so if I had a doctor's appointment or had to go somewhere else, I had to take William to work and then go back and get him. Our lives were routine as we looked forward to our first child.

When I was expecting my first baby, the creative thread in me would not let me send out store-bought announcements. On one of those long days of waiting, I sat down and wrote the birth announcement for my little boy. Since I felt so thankful that God had allowed my husband and me to have this child, I considered him a gift from heaven:

A Gift from Heaven

We received a gift from heaven
And thought you'd like to know.
It's small and neat and mighty sweet

And something that will grow!
Of course, the first thing that we did
Was check on all its parts.
It has two arms, two legs, two ears, and two eyes
As bright as little tarts.
And then as I looked closer
I noticed there's no hair;
I guess I shouldn't worry
But the child just looks so bare!
I guess I've got a lot to learn
About a tiny babe,
I just know it's the cutest thing,
Regardless of how it's made.
So thanks, dear Lord, for this blessed gift,
That's bright as the rising sun.
We'll cherish it and love it—
For it's our own precious one.

On the back of the card, I printed "Father's First Thought." William's thoughts were rather different from mine. Being an engineer and dealing with numbers, he viewed our new family member as a tax deduction, so I printed a ten-dollar bill and put the baby's statistics on it with a baby's head in the center of the bill!

William really was so attentive to me, but his work was long, hard, and very demanding. He was dedicated to learning his new job, and Milliken sent him off quite often to a school or training update.

Within about three days of my due date, right after William left to go to work, I started feeling different. I began to feel some contractions, but, never having had a baby before, I didn't know exactly if this was the real thing or not. I just waited it out until William came home around six.

I had been miserable all day. William called the doctor, and the doctor said to bring me on to the hospital. This was a small hospital, and it did not have the latest or most up-to-date equipment. I was hurting so badly by this time that I was in tears, so the doctor broke my water. Then, through much pain and tribulation, I had a big boy. Since I have always had a slim body, this large baby was very difficult for me to birth. The gynecologist I was under did not believe in a lot of medication, and I learned later that this was why it was so hard for me.

William was both tickled and thankful for a healthy baby. We named him William Todd. Our lives certainly changed when we took Todd home!

The lady next door to us lived alone But she had a lot of visitors and there was often an 18-wheeler truck parked in her yard. We shared a double drive, so this made it hard for us to have room to drive in and out. She was very nice to talk to, but it was not unusual for us to hear an argument and loud noises coming from her home, especially late at night.

About a year after we were there, William went out to go to work and discovered our car was gone. Needless to say, he was quite upset. We called the police and went through filling out a report, and about a week later our car was found in another state with some damage. We realized we needed to move to a neighborhood more conducive to living with a toddler.

My parents became so concerned about all this that they wanted to help us financially so we could find another place to live. We moved out of town, about five miles, since houses were cheaper there, and the man selling the house was a Christian and really wanted to help us out. The house was much nicer and the neighborhood was pretty. William had farther to travel to work, but we were thankful for such a nice neighborhood.

We enjoyed the First Baptist Church in Hartsville. The people just took us under their wing. William and I worked with the young people. I worked with the Girl's Auxiliary, known as G. A's. and children's choir. We had the first G.A. coronation the church had ever had. It was so meaningful.

When Todd was three years old, we were blessed with another child, a little girl. So I wrote the second birth announcement: I wrote it through the eyes of my son.

Shan't Say a Word

We have a secret, my Teddy and me,
And I shan't tell it, not even to thee.
I told the Teddy but can't tell the bee,
'Cause things might get buzzing round my house, you see!!
I'll give you a hint if you have to know,
It's about my mom and her actions that show—
She's getting ready for something, I think,
And I'm 'fraid I'll tell it as quick as a wink.
It sure seemed funny when she moved my bed,
She went through my drawers, and strangely she said,
"Now you must be sweet and learn how to share.
And not treat your sister as rough as a bear!!"
One day I noticed the wash on the line:
The diaper, the booties, the blanket—all mine!!
They are all so tiny, too tiny for me,
I'm gonna ask Mom to explain things, you see.
She looked out the window at a little bird's nest,
Explaining to me—Oh, I shan't tell the rest.
And yet we know what the secret's about—
That tree and the nest and those things that fly out.
What still puzzles me is that lacy pink dress,
How things in this world can get in a mess.
That wash on the line—Oh, I shan't say a word—
When Mom fits that dress right onto that bird.

Todd was not thrilled at first with the new baby, Robyn. Later, as she became big enough to play with him, they became the typical brother and sister companions.

Not long after Robyn was born, William was transferred to Lavonia, Georgia. We went to Lavonia and looked around and it seemed such a desolate place with not much to offer. Since William is from Anderson and his parents were living there, we decided to live in Anderson, and William commuted to Lavonia. William and I both agreed that it was better for me to be a stay-at-home mom and use my teaching degree with my own children before I went back to teaching. So I spent my time with the children during their preschool years, preparing them for school.

William and I joined his home church in Anderson, which pleased his parents. We did most anything and everything in that little church. William was a deacon and chaired many church committees. Both our children came to know the Lord at this small church and were very much involved. When my kids were younger, I tried to get in some extra learning with them during the summer months. In the morning before any of us got started with the day's activities, I would do some educational activities on their level, read books, and have a devotional with them. At night, we read our Bibles together and had prayer together. When they got a little older and were in different evening activities, they did their own daily Bible reading and prayer.

My son accepted Christ at a very young age, but he had talked with the pastor and knew what he was doing. Robyn was a little older. I walked in her room one night and she had her Bible out. She knew that I wanted her to accept Christ. Sure enough, she did, and I was so proud of both of my children.

ROBYN'S RACE

I love experiencing God,
Knowing he's close
And watching me the most, caring for me,
And I love you too!!
I love Raggedy Ann and Andy,
Scooby Doo and vanilla milkshakes
And I love you, too!

CHAPTER 3

DELIGHT

I RETURNED TO classroom teaching when Robyn was in kindergarten. I taught at the school she attended so I could have the same
hours she had. When she was in second grade, I took a full-time job at
a very good elementary school in Anderson.

I served as choir director at our church for sixteen years, even while
teaching full-time in Anderson schools. I was privileged to have my
husband, son, and Robyn in the choir. They kept me on my toes and
let me know what they liked and disliked.

Robyn was entertaining and had a quick wit. One evening while
rehearsing, we heard a commotion in the back of the church. There
were very noisy sounds of laughter and talking. I asked one of the choir
members to see if that was Robyn causing the uproar. Sure enough, it
was none other than my daughter. On another rehearsal evening, I passed
out a rather difficult anthem and was trying hard to get each harmony
part across to the choir. After ten minutes or so, everyone was getting
frustrated. Robyn stood up and said, "OK, everybody, let's pass this
baby in." Her remark relieved the tension immediately. Everyone in our
small church knew Robyn and loved it when she was around because
there was never a dull moment.

Robyn had many interests. In high school she was in the orchestra and played violin. (I couldn't believe she wanted to do this—it was out of character for her.) We rented a violin for a while to see if she was going to stick with it. She surprised us and began to get better, so we bought her a nicer one. With her lively personality and jovial attitude, we didn't think she would keep on playing, but she did. She also was on the varsity basketball team that won a state championship during her junior year. Needless to say, the team spent many hours practicing each week.

I remember one day she came home from school and I was making a large batch of hash for company. This is an all-day cook-a-thon, but it feeds a crowd of people and is tasty. It takes six pounds of beef and three pounds of onions, and I thought the house smelled good. However, the onions had a rather pungent smell. Robyn was home long enough to dress for practice and eat a sandwich and then she headed back to school. When she returned home several hours later, she said, "Mama, you can't make hash anymore when I'm going back to school because the whole team said I smelled like onions. It was all in my hair and my clothes." Robyn tried hard to keep me straight on what I should and should not do!

We had an old station wagon that we used to transport Robyn back and forth to all her activities. She claimed it, and when I needed it, guess where it was? With Robyn! During this time she also had fallen in love with a movie star named Tom Selleck, and she pasted his picture on the dashboard of the wagon. This didn't make the rest of us too happy when we had to use this car, but it was a delight to her. Everything Robyn did was with enthusiasm.

Robyn wanted to try out for drum major of the marching band for her senior year in high school. Her orchestra leader told her he didn't see how she could possibly schedule her courses, basketball, orchestra, and band. The rehearsals were sometimes at the same hour. But she loved to direct music and had the background to do it.

She got some help to set up a routine for the tryout. The day she tried out, William was in the hospital undergoing hernia surgery. Robyn came to the hospital with some of her friends after tryouts because she couldn't wait to tell us she was the new drum major for the coming year at Hanna High School! I was totally surprised, as I had no idea she would get the position.

Robyn informed me she was responsible for obtaining her own drum major outfit and boots, hats, and gloves. After inquiring around and looking at several outfits, we found a lady who made things like this. We talked with her and decided to go with two different outfits—a white one trimmed in gold with a white hat, and a black, less dressy outfit with a vest and white, big-sleeved blouse with black hat and boots. The first time Robyn performed, I was tremendously proud of her. She looked beautiful and did a good job, and she was on "cloud nine." I wished Tom Selleck could have seen her! She had accomplished a dream and had figured out a way to stay in the orchestra and band and also play basketball.

When Robyn decided she would go to Anderson College, which was in the same town we lived in, she informed us she would not live at home because she wanted to be involved in campus life and couldn't do that if she stayed home. It didn't surprise us one bit that she wanted to be involved—after all, we lived with her!

Robyn was very much involved at Anderson and loved every minute of it. She was in the AC Choir, president of campus ministries, secretary of Fellowship of Christian Athletes, on the freshmen and sophomore senate, a member of the Denmark Society, student assistant for the Spanish professor, and she was selected to go with a small group of students on a mission trip to Bermuda. She was also in *Who's Who Among American Students.*

Just before she graduated from Anderson, she walked into the office of the vice president, who knew her quite well. He asked her what she was going to do after she graduated. She told him she was coming back to Anderson to have his job!

Robyn decided she wanted to go into social work, and someone told her about an outstanding program at Presbyterian College in South Carolina and recommended she go and talk to the head of the department. She did this, and afterward she felt this was where she should go next.

During Robyn's second year at Presbyterian, someone told her about a girl whom no one wanted to room with. Robyn said, "Oh, I'll room with her." She turned out to be a very nice young woman and very attractive. Her personality was very different from Robyn's, but they were brought close together when the roommate's brother was killed in an accident on a ski trip only a month after she and Robyn became roommates. Robyn helped her through this tragic time, and went to her home and to the funeral although she did not know the boy. Robyn always reached out to anyone who was hurting.

After they both graduated, Robyn's roommate asked Robyn to be in her wedding. She was marrying the son of the governor of Georgia.

We were invited to Georgia's governor's mansion, where all the bridesmaids were staying. We felt very intimidated about driving up to the mansion in an old station wagon with Tom Selleck's picture on the dashboard! Someone parked our wagon, and Robyn met us at the door with a big smile and said, "Hey, Mom and Dad. Come on in. I want you to meet the governor." I loved every minute of this unique experience, seeing the beautiful mansion and the gorgeous decorations, and experiencing the southern hospitality. But my husband was glad when it was over! He was not a socialite.

Needless to say, Robyn loved being with people. When she came home from college, the phone was always ringing and young people filled the house constantly. I never knew how many of her friends to expect: two, four, or ten! One day, she called me from school and said a young man was coming home with her (whom she really liked), and she wanted to fix him a steak supper. I had to be at a PTA meeting in about thirty minutes. Robyn wanted to know what to do and how to do it, where the food was, and how long each step would take. Now, she had never been one to follow me around in the kitchen; she was involved in too many activities to learn how to cook. But I gave her directions, and she took it from there.

Robyn thrived on doing new things and always accepted a challenge. Her take-charge personality sometimes surprised even me. Another weekend she called and said she was coming home and bringing this same young man with her. I was in the kitchen cooking while they played a game when he got up to be excused and a short time later yelled from the bathroom that the toilet paper was out. Robyn didn't even hesitate—she ran down the hall, grabbed a new roll, opened the bathroom door, and threw it in! I almost fainted.

Many of Robyn's best friendships were made at Presbyterian College. They were all so close and had similar interests. A group of them regularly went out to eat together, played games together, and visited in each other's homes. There were four boys in this group and about six girls, and I was impressed with each one of them.

Robyn had a favorite doll—a handmade Raggedy Ann that her grandmother had given her when she was about eight years old. When Robyn went to Anderson College, Raggedy Ann was one of the first things she packed. When Robyn left Anderson, Raggedy Ann was looking a little worn, but she went to Presbyterian College, stayed on Robyn's bed, and slept with her each night.

Some of Robyn's close friends (especially the boys) decided to play a trick on her one day. When Robyn came in from class, Raggedy Ann was not on the bed. When Robyn missed her, she panicked. She was a resident assistant for the hall at this time, and all the girls thought they were going to have to go to the president to get help locating Raggedy Ann. Those boys were watching everything that was going on and having a glorious laugh. When they figured Robyn was not going to give up, was not going to bed without Raggedy Ann, and had alarmed the entire campus, the boys "found" Raggedy Ann. They understood Robyn's determination.

Besides being a dorm Resident Assistant, Robyn was in the college choir and Fellowship of Christian Athletes; she was a member of the Presbyterian College Student Admissions Advisory Council, and a Big Sister to a Thornwell High School student. It seemed she feared missing any opportunity, but she made a difference at Presbyterian College.

Robyn was never home in the summer during these years; she was busy preparing herself for what she wanted to do in life. One summer she was youth director at Riverstreet Baptist Church. The next summer she was youth director at Central Presbyterian Church and an instructor at the Children's Learning Center in Anderson. One summer she was a youth counselor at the YMCA. After she graduated from Presbyterian College, she went to Mentone, Alabama, to Saddle Rock Camp for Girls as a counselor. She savored each experience and learned from each one.

CHAPTER 4

SEMINARY YEARS

WHEN ROBYN GRADUATED from Presbyterian College with her Bachelor of Science degree in Sociology, she wanted to continue her education at seminary level and obtain a Master in Social Work degree. I found the following paper in her things that she had packed up:

> God has given me a Christian family, without whom I would not be where I am today. God continues to bless my life every day, and I know that he is real and that he is preparing me for the job he has for me to do. I believe that seminary is where the Lord is leading me at this point in my life. To be effective at what he wants me to do, I know that a masters degree is needed. The Lord is at the center of my life. My goal, always, is to be in his will and be the best servant I can be in his kingdom.

Robyn said she knew she wanted to go to Southern Baptist Theological Seminary in Louisville, Kentucky. Now, William had felt we could breathe a sigh of financial relief when she finished Presbyterian College. We had made payments to two private schools for her and her brother for a year. However, we were behind her 100 percent and wanted to support her decision, as she felt led. My husband mapped out the way to Kentucky and off we went. Robyn took notes all the way, because she knew with her daddy's job and my teaching she would probably be traveling back and forth by herself most of the time. It was hard for me to miss school, and William's work at Milliken was very demanding.

Life with Robyn was never dull, and she was always planning for the future. As we neared Louisville, we began to hear a shrill, continuous noise. The closer we got, the louder it grew. My husband stopped the car and got out to see if it could be the car. Immediately, flying bugs were all around him, and we realized every tree was surrounded by them, flapping their wings and buzzing. When we got into Louisville, we were informed it was hatching-out season for the cicada bugs. Every seven years, cicadas hatch out and live for three weeks—and we happened to be there when this happened. Lucky us! It was like a movie—bugs everywhere making that loud, awful noise. They were all over the roads, yards, and fields. It was quite a welcome to Kentucky!

After touring the campus at Southern Seminary, we checked out several places off campus where Robyn might want to live. None particularly appealed to her or to us, and some were not in a good section of town for a young woman, so she decided to room on campus.

After making several major decisions with her concerning seminary life, we bid the cicadas and the seminary farewell. We all returned home and Robyn spent the rest of the summer at home, working as a youth director at a local church.

Robyn knew we were behind her and would continue to pay her way as we could. We knew the Lord would help us. She did not have a car at this time, but since she was going so far, we gave her the best car we had so we would feel better about her safety. We all felt as though she was in God's will, and we wanted her to be prepared for whatever God had in store for her. We knew she had the talent to make a tremendous contribution to his work and that she had more willpower and determination than either of us possessed.

Robyn returned to Southern Seminary in the fall, and how I hated to see her pack up and drive off for that long trip alone. Her dad helped her again with directions to be sure she knew where she was going. The Lord was with her and she was blessed with a compatible roommate upon her arrival. Of course, she entered joyfully into seminary life with all the zest for living that she had always had. She made so many wonderful friends and they became just like family. One day I called her and the answering machine came on and said, "I'm not here. I've gone out with Tom Selleck, and I'll call you when I get back." Robyn loved a good laugh. You never knew what you might hear if you called her and got her machine.

One of her favorite foods was spaghetti; she would not eat it at a restaurant because she said it did not compare to mine. One night she called from the seminary and said, "Poopsie, tell me how to make spaghetti, just like you make it. I am having the gang over to eat and I am cooking." I nearly fainted. Robyn was not usually in the kitchen. However, these were her friends, and friends meant the world to Robyn. I gave her the recipe and explained in detail what to do. She called back to tell me how successful she was, how everyone enjoyed the meal, and how proud of herself she was for cooking. (I was proud of her too.)

One summer when she came home for a long weekend, she told me she had a friend getting married at Pretty Place, an outdoor chapel at a campground in the mountains. She wanted to go and asked me to go with her. I had no idea where Pretty Place was, but off we went. We almost never found it. The road went round and round in the mountains, so much so that we thought we might lose everything we had eaten the past week.

Finally we arrived at the campground and found the chapel, and I was awestruck. I thought to myself, as I sat there looking out over the edge of a mountain against the most beautiful background of God's handiwork, that no decorator or florist could attempt that artwork or that matchless beauty. It was a little glimpse of heaven.

It was a special outdoor wedding and a special day. The music was simple but beautiful. The open-front chapel was placed over the edge of the mountain. The mountains wrapped all the way around the front of the chapel as far as the eye could see. The brush of a gentle breeze, a woodsy aroma, birds flying by, lush greenery, clouds of blue, and God's beautiful heavens hovered over us and gave us a sense of worship that engulfed us as we observed God's quiet presence.

Robyn and I were both touched deeply by Pretty Place. I was so touched that when my son decided to get married four years later after losing Robyn, he and his finance, Sylvia couldn't decide what church they wanted to be married in so I said to them, "I know somewhere I would like you to go and just see how you like it." When they went, their minds were made up. I was even more touched as they stood out there in front of that chapel overhang, looking over those beautiful mountains with one huge cross at the altar behind them. In the background, God's handiwork proclaimed "How Great Thou Art"! Robyn would have been so pleased with the lovely Christian lady Todd married and especially choosing Pretty Place as their sanctuary. I regret Robyn did not have the privilege of knowing her sister-in-law.

As we looked out over the overhang, we read the engraved marker on the stone wall: "We must never forget that the land and the waters are entrusted to us for the moment only, that following generations must live from that land and drink of that water. It is not enough just to leave something for them: as God's stewards, we must leave it all better than we found it."—Louis L'Amour.

Another marker read, "Do not follow where the path may lead. Go, instead, where there is no path and leave a trail." Robyn left many trails.

At Southern Seminary, true to her character, Robyn put her name down for some jobs outside the seminary to make some extra money. This helped us out some with her gas bill, as it was fairly high most months. She drove to her jobs as youth director of Highland Park Baptist Church and as a social worker at Spring Meadow Children's Home. She had to provide her own transportation to and from the Highland Park church, and since the church did not have a van or a bus, she drove her car and transported youth in it to different events. On top of all this, she had a job as a nanny.

Sharon Calkins, who lived in Louisville about ten miles from the seminary and whose husband worked for Winn Dixie, called the seminary and asked for a list of names of students they would recommend as a nanny. Mrs. Calkins chose Robyn because her name was spelled with a *y*. Her only child was a three-year-old named Jonathan.

When Robyn went to meet the family, the event was like cake and ice cream. Robyn had always loved children and been good with them, and Mrs. Calkins just fell in love with her and hired her on the spot. Now, when I say "hired her," Mrs. Calkins really wanted a live-in babysitter, but the job turned out to be a welcome relief for Robyn as a home away from home. The Calkins family just adopted her and treated her like a daughter. Mrs. Calkins loaned Robyn her car, had parties at her home for Robyn's gang from the seminary, and loved the entertainment Robyn provided with all the activities.

Robyn and Jonathan got along very well because Robyn entertained him from the time she got there until the time she left. She would call me and tell me all the things Jonathan could do and how smart he was and what he was reading. I thought she was exaggerating, but it ended up she wasn't; he was an exceptional child. Jonathan wrote Robyn love notes, even at three years old. Their relationship was so special that when my son got married four years after Robyn passed away we asked Jonathan to be an honorary groomsman at Todd's wedding to represent Robyn.

Robyn's masters program was a four-year degree, but Robyn planned to obtain it in three-and-a-half years. She had a little problem with this because the seminary offered only limited courses in the summers. She took more hours in the fall and winter terms to acquire required subjects and attended the January term—an extra term between the winter and spring quarters. Robyn also had a tendency to overload herself with work outside the seminary. She seldom got to come home; in the summers she stayed in Louisville to work. We were paying all her expenses, even gas, although she tried to help out as much as she could. Even with all these activities going on in her life, she managed to stay on track with her course work.

Robyn wanted us to visit during the summer after her first year at Southern Seminary to meet her friends and the Calkins family. She suggested we stay in the seminary guest room to be closer to her and see her friends. I thought that sounded good—"seminary guest room." We took Robyn and her friends out for supper, and there wasn't a dull moment with all they had to share with us. But after driving all day and being entertained by Robyn and her friends, I was looking forward to a good night's sleep in the guest room.

What a laugh it was! Low to the floor, the bed was like a pigs' trough and not much bigger. When you got in it, everything rolled to the middle. In no way could we make it level. Now, I liked being close to my husband, but when the bed closed in around me and I couldn't pry myself uphill, the situation became aggravating and not restful. What a night! The next morning Robyn came bounding down the hall to get us to go for breakfast. I asked her if she had ever noticed anything unusual about the seminary beds. My husband and I figured out that beds did not matter to the students because they spent very little time in them! We enjoyed our visit and especially being with Robyn and all her friends, and this camaraderie was so special to Robyn.

Robyn was to graduate in December. An orphanage in St. Louis, the Missouri Baptist Children's Home, interviewed her and showed a lot of interest in her. They told her if she worked there for two years she would receive extra certification on her master's degree in social work, qualifying her for more money. We were hoping she would get a job closer to home, and she promised she would after the two years were completed. She also interviewed at Thornwell Home for Children in Clinton, South Carolina, across from Presbyterian College. I went with her and studied in the library while she interviewed. Thornwell wanted to hire her that day, but she would not commit and promised to respond later. After much prayer, she decided to go to St. Louis.

Several weeks after Robyn committed to Missouri Baptist Children's Home, she learned they were so impressed with her that they wanted her to be in charge of a new home on their campus for unwed mothers. Robyn was elated at this opportunity. One of her friends from the seminary was hired at this same orphanage, and they decided to get an apartment together. It looked as if things were really working out for Robyn, and we felt good about her rooming with someone she knew.

Top left: Robyn and
her brother, Todd.

Robyn, in High
School-Senior picture

Bermuda

Three AC Students Will Lead Crusade

Special to the Independent-Mail

Three Anderson College students from Anderson will be spending 10 days in Bermuda this month, not to enjoy a summer vacation but to participate in a missions team.

While on the island, the trio will minister at a small church and lead a youth crusade.

Robyn Axmann, Amy Hopkins and Jan Roberts are among eight AC freshmen selected to participate in the project, which begins Friday, according to the AC News Service.

This is the third year the college has sent a missions team to Bermuda. The trip was arranged by the Rev. and Mrs. Reginald Hill, native South Carolinians, and one of three missionary couples in Bermuda sponsored by the AC Campus Ministries Department.

Sandy Kidd, director of AC Campus Ministries, said students are responsible for just about every aspect of the trip, including costs for transportation, food and spending money.

"The students are planning cooperative fund-raising activities," Kidd said. "They will try to raise money in their home churches and through various fund-raising projects at the college. To save expenses, each student will take a sleeping bag and stay in a church building, as well as cook their own meals."

Kidd, who also serves as chaplain at AC, and Dr. Jim Whitlow, director of the AC Counseling Center, will accompany the students to Bermuda.

Each student is attending musical and worship clinics, evangelism training, personal witnessing seminars and an orientation session on Bermuda.

"I hope the team will be brought closer together and that all of us can learn from God and each other through our experiences," said Miss Axmann, one of three T.L. Hanna High graduates in the group.

Hoping to do her share of evangelism, Miss Roberts said she believes the trip will be meaningful.

"In our effort to reach out to others, each of us will become stronger in our faith and in our witnessing," she said.

Miss Axmann and Miss Roberts have done missions work before.

The trip will be a first-time experience for Miss Hopkins.

The daughter of Mr. and Mrs. William

AC News Service Photo

Sandy Kidd, Anderson College Campus Ministries director, shows a map of Bermuda to three AC freshmen, Robyn Axmann, Jan Roberts and Amy Hopkins. Dr. Jim Whitlow, AC counselor, will accompany the students on a crusade to the island.

R. Axmann, Miss Axmann is a member of Mountain Creek Baptist Church. At AC, she was on the freshman senate and was recently elected to the sophomore senate. She is a member of Baptist Young Women, Church Related Vocations, Gamma Beta Phi, Student Alumni Association and the Student Government Association Social Board.

A member of Anderson's First Baptist Church, Miss Hopkins is the daughter of Dr. and Mrs. Mark Hopkins. At AC, she is a member of the choir, Radiance, Pep Band, Phi Theta Kappa and Gamma Beta Phi. She also participates in various plays produced by the theatre department.

Miss Roberts, a member of Boulevard Baptist Church, is the daughter of Dr. and Mrs. Richard Roberts. At AC, she is a member of the Journey Team, choir and Phi Theta Kappa.

31

SHE WON THE RACE

Robyn fourth from the bottom at the
Governor's Mansion in Georgia

Pretty Place Chapel

My son's wedding at Pretty Place

Pretty Place—My son's wedding

My son at Pretty Place

My son's wedding-Jonathan-(far right) the child Robyn was Nanny for in Seminary

Parties at Jonathan's House with "the gang" from the seminary

Denna, her room mate at Seminary

DEAR, ROBYN I MISS YOU SO
MUCH I'D LIKE YOU TO COME
VISIT ME SOMEDAY. I LOVE YOU
VERY MUCH. I PLAYED IN THE
SNOW I WENT ON THE SLED BY
MYSELF. I HAD FUN IN
DECEMBER AND NOW IT'S
JANUARY IN 1991.

LOVE,
JONATHAN

Mom & Dad,   4/16/90

Thanks so much for
coming this past week.
I can't begin to tell you
how much it meant to
me. Throyt everything
that has happened this
past week it again makes
me so thankful for both
of you. God has truly blessed
me w/ wonderful, caring
parents. I am who I
am because of the love
you have given me. The
words "thank you" do not begin
to express enoyt appreciation.
I love you both,
Robyn

Robyn and
friends

Stacy, in middle, her room
mate at Anderson College.

Brook in middle, married
the governor's son.

Robyn and Romona, the girl she
was to room with in St. Louis.

Robyn, Dr. Garland, Romona.

Axmann Leads CM

By Barry Bradley

CM President Robyn Axmann

Robyn Axmann will be leading AC's Campus Ministries Program as president for the 1984-85 year.

Axmann will be replacing Debra Scott as this years president.

Her main goal for the new year is to have more student involvement in the programs, as well as having more felllowships.

"I feel God has put me here specifically. I know I'm doing the right thing. I hope to grow more spiritually as a result," she said.

Further Axmann stated, "I hope to better campus ministries. I hope to help anyone as well as I can and make myself available for all."

Other CM leaders elected were Tania Gray, Baptist Young Women, Larry Pitts, Church Related Vocations, Len Solesbee and Mary Wimmer, Outreach, and Angie Hogsed, Journey Teams.

Also Andy Perry, Mission and Social Action, Susan Smith, Publicity, Kim Kincade, women's Agape, and Angie Nicholson, Sunshine Friends.

These Campus ministries leaders were nominated by last year's CM leaders and were officially inducted into their positions on April 4 in the Fine Art Center on leadership installation day.

Ellen and Robyn, took the Senior Citizens
in Louisville to the Convention.

Friend at the
Seminary.

Robyn digging foundation for new
building at Children's Home.

CHAPTER 5

DOUBLE VISION

A S ROBYN WAS finishing up her work at Highland Park Church as
youth director, the church asked her to accompany a group of senior
citizens to the Southern Baptist Convention. Robyn and Ellen Seacrest,
a friend from the seminary, went to New Orleans for the convention
with this group of lively members from Highland Park. The church
paid all their expenses. Ellen and Robyn were both very outgoing and
fun loving. They were ready for a great trip.

When Robyn called to tell us they had arrived safely, she said that
in the Superdome her head did not feel right. I remembered that several
weeks prior to this she had been out jogging and suddenly felt so weak
that she had to sit down on the curb. She couldn't even make it back to
campus by herself; someone who knew her came along and got her back
to school. I thought that she had overloaded herself with activities and
seminary work and was just worn out. I continued to have a listening
ear and cautioned her about overdoing.

William and I decided we would send her a plane ticket to join
us for a week at the beach that summer before she was to graduate in
December. We got to be with her so seldom and always tried to make

plans around her school calendar. She had always loved the beach and agreed this was a great idea and brought a friend with her.

About the third day at the beach, she told me she was beginning to see double. I immediately called my brother, who was a pharmacist in Spartanburg, and asked him to make an appointment with a good ophthalmologist for the day of our return. He could not get an appointment on such short notice, but when we got back, I contacted another doctor, who agreed to see her before we put her on the plane back to Louisville. When he examined her, however, I could tell he had no idea what the problem was.

By this time Robyn's left eye was beginning to turn in toward her nose. I was so concerned and really did not want her to return to Louisville. Of course, she was determined to go back. Her flight was the next day, but she promised us she would schedule an appointment with an ophthalmologist as soon as she got back to the seminary. I was upset by this time, fearing that something was physically wrong with her. I'll never forget my strong emotions while putting her on the plane. She went to the little window and waved to us. I just said a prayer as the plane lifted off the runway: "God, please take care of her and help us find the problem."

The doctor she saw when she returned in Louisville told her that she had always had a weak eye and it was just now showing up. He said the other eye was trying to compensate for the weakness and he would put prisms on her glasses to correct the problem. The first set of prisms made her see much better, and she said she was not seeing double. We all were excited about the results.

However, after about two weeks, Robyn was seeing double again. The doctor put stronger prisms on her glasses and also consulted his mentor, who confirmed the diagnosis but also suggested a CAT scan. The CAT scan did not show anything unusual, but Robyn's eyesight was getting worse. In just two more weeks, the double vision returned again, and the doctor put his strongest set of prisms on her glasses.

Robyn's eyesight was challenging her. The lack of answers was challenging me.

Robyn was trying to finish up the last of her classes at the seminary and her work at Spring Meadows Children's Home, and also was corresponding with the Missouri Baptist Children's Home about her job there. Her apartment in St. Louis was unfurnished, so she and her roommate were trying to figure out how they would furnish it.

She was to finish her coursework the first week in August and wanted us to come and move her to St. Louis. We took William's small Mazda pickup and headed to Louisville. How excited we were about Robyn's future!

I went to the doctor with her when we got to Louisville, and he assured us he was doing the right thing. We even talked about surgery to correct the eye that was moving toward her nose. He was going to send her to the doctor he had studied under to do the surgery. So Robyn's plan was to go ahead and move to St. Louis and return to Louisville later to see the doctor she'd been referred to about doing the surgery. I could tell Robyn was concerned, but she looked on the bright side of everything and did not let anything depress her. She was about to attain her goal—to complete her MSW and start serving the Lord in the job she had been preparing herself for.

I still was not feeling good about all this And now I noticed that Robyn's voice sounded slightly different. I asked her if she also had noticed it, and she said she had.

We packed and packed. Robyn never threw anything away. William was an excellent packer, but you can get just so much in a pickup truck and a Sierra Oldsmobile.

Our den furniture was about sixteen years old, and Robyn had suggested that we bring the couch to her and get ourselves a new one. I thought that was a good idea, and the couch was on the truck. We decided that all the boxes, TV, air conditioning unit, clothes for all seasons, and books were not going to fit in a pickup truck with a couch.

We talked about renting a U-Haul; however, neither the truck nor our Oldsmobile had a trailer hitch. William started talking about what we could leave behind.

Now, Robyn was very sentimental and cared about everything. Since she had acquired the Calkins family as a second family in Louisville, she suggested we take a load over to their house and store things there until she could get them at a later date. We took a load over and left it in the basement there.

One of the things we left behind was the air conditioning unit. Its history was another example of a beautiful friendship. Robyn's roommate at Anderson College, Stacy, was like a sister to Robyn. When Robyn was corresponding with her from the seminary and telling her how hot her room was, Stacy said she had an extra unit stored that Robyn could use. She brought it to us and Robyn took it back with her after a weekend home. It was all we could do to squeeze it into the trunk of her car, and off she went. None of her friends at the seminary knew how to install an air conditioning unit, but they helped her get it in and running. They even accomplished this task on the second floor! We had to figure out a way to get that borrowed air conditioning unit back to Stacy in South Carolina. Someone told Robyn she could store it for a short time in the basement of the seminary; that's what we did.

Finally, loaded to the hilt, we headed for St. Louis. Only my husband had room to sit on the driver's seat of his truck, and Robyn and I barely squeezed into the car. We drove very carefully since we were so loaded down, and Robyn had directions for us once we got into St. Louis.

We were looking forward to seeing Ramona, Robyn's friend and new roommate. A little older than Robyn, Ramona had finished at the seminary the year before. She was the daughter of home missionaries and was bearing most of her own expenses. We were so happy for Robyn to have someone to room with in St. Louis whom she already knew was a fine Christian girl. Ramona met us at a service station in St. Louis and we followed her on to the apartment. After our five-hour drive to

St. Louis, we attempted to carry the couch up a flight of stairs with all the other stuff. The apartment was on the second floor and we got a lot of exercise.

The next day we went furniture shopping. We had told Robyn that for graduation we would give her a bedroom suite for the new apartment. After several hours, we had a beautiful suite that was to be delivered the next morning. Robyn was so excited about beginning her career and having a nice apartment near her work.

School was starting in Spartanburg where I taught and I needed to be there, so William and I left early the next morning. Our hearts were heavy because we were still deeply concerned about Robyn's sight. It was a long trip back to South Carolina in more ways than one. Robyn stayed at the new apartment, waiting on the new bedroom suite.

The next day, nothing would do but for her to arrange her room the way she wanted it. She placed her clothes in the drawers and put the new coverlet and pillows on her bed. She placed the lamps. I was going to do curtains at home and send them later. She had so much fun fixing up her own space.

That same afternoon, Robyn was to head back to Louisville. She could not drive without wearing a patch (she did not let us know this until later), so Ramona patched her eye, and with her usual determination Robyn drove herself back to Kentucky.

About three weeks later, Robyn again returned to Louisville to see the surgeon, and Mrs. Calkins went with her. Late that afternoon, Mrs. Calkins called me and said for us to come to Louisville—Robyn had a more serious problem and the doctor was sending her to the hospital for an MRI. I got so upset I could hardly tell my husband over the telephone. We both arranged to get time off work to go back to Louisville.

I called my son to tell him what we were doing and why, and he could not believe it, knowing Robyn and her busy life as we had all known her growing up. He tried to soothe my feelings, telling me, "Mom, Robyn's not sick." I assured him that she was but we didn't know yet what was wrong.

We had already planned to head to Louisville if Robyn had surgery, but now we were faced with something different. We had expected minor surgery to clip a muscle to bring the eye back in and correct the double vision.

It was a long drive to Louisville this time.

DIAGNOSIS

ROBYN TRIED TO be in good spirits and had made reservations for us at a motel in Louisville. She went to the motel with us, and I could tell she was uptight about what might be wrong with her eye.

She had already had the MRI when we arrived, and we were to see the doctor for a conference. We thought he would call us and let us know when to come; he had the number of the motel where we were staying. He did not know Robyn or us and evidently did not know or feel what we were feeling at this time.

After we called the doctor's office numerous times, he finally called the motel where we were. Over the phone he told me that the MRI showed a lesion on the brain stem. He wanted us to make plans to take Robyn to a large teaching hospital and suggested four for us to consider. He wanted us to think about our options and then call him back, and I said I would.

Robyn was sitting on the other bed in the motel room and could tell by my reaction and my voice that what the doctor was saying was not something she wanted to hear. Tears began to roll down her cheeks. I was upset over not only what I was hearing but by how uncaring it seemed for the doctor not to talk with us face-to-face.

After William, Robyn, and I discussed it, we decided to go to Duke University. We had heard so many good things about Duke, and it was closer to Spartanburg than the other choices. I called the doctor back and told him of our decision, and he made an appointment with a brain surgeon at Duke for the next week. We took all of Robyn's records from Louisville with us.

It was a traumatic experience for Robyn to leave Louisville, like tearing her heart out. We went back to the seminary to get a few things she had left there. Almost everything else we had taken to Louisville or to Mrs. Calkins's home. Robyn had not cleaned out her desk at Spring Meadow Children's Home and had left some personal things over there. When I mentioned going by and doing this, I could tell it was more than she wanted to face at the time. None of us wanted to talk about it. She decided she would ask one of her friends to go over there for her and do that after we left town. Robyn had so many friends there; the staff and personnel had fallen in love with her, as had the children. She had worked there for almost a year. Although the seminary did not allow students to work full-time while working on a degree, the personnel director called the seminary and asked for special permission for Robyn to work full-time if she felt she could do it, and the seminary agreed. She told us so often of her work and going to the homes to visit and the things she was faced with concerning home environments. William and I had to pray a little harder for her protection and wisdom and time. We just had to thank God for the opportunities she had and ask him to give her the ability and strength to carry through with her studies.

The long trip home was hard. We talked about all the activities she had been in and put her future in God's hands, knowing he would heal whatever the problem was at this time. We tried to assure her that God was with us and would take care of her.

We both got off work again and took Robyn to Duke. After finding our way around, we finally saw the neurosurgeon. He wanted to run another MRI and would show the results to a panel of doctors to see if the brain stem did have something on it, and he wanted to run a series of tests, starting with the simplest and moving to the most difficult, to eliminate all the things the lesion could be. He had Robyn do several things related to her eyes and balance and then sent us to another doctor to rule out myasthenia gravis.

In the waiting room, I read the symptoms of MG, and Robyn had every one of them. The doctor did several tests with her and suggested a spinal tap, and Robyn agreed right there. After these tests, the doctor said she did not have MG, so we were to return for another day of testing. Nothing showed up on those tests either. We were given an appointment for a cerebral angiogram and several other tests a few days later.

The second MRI confirmed a lesion on the brain stem, but exactly what it was hadn't been determined. After eliminating everything that had been suspected, the neurosurgeon said the last thing left to do was a biopsy. He explained to us this was very dangerous and would take several hours. Though he would take only a pinhead sample from the lesion, one mistake could cause extreme disabilities, because so many bodily functions are controlled by the brain stem. The surgery could paralyze her or take away her ability to speak or any number of other functions if things did not go right.

They would shave her hair up to her ears; this broke my heart because Robyn had beautiful, long black hair she could wear many different ways. But that was minor now if it took this to identify the problem.

We knew we had a body of people praying. I knew God was with us. As Robyn was rolled out on a stretcher, I ran and kissed her and told her we were praying. Robyn seemed to have a peace about her that William and I did not have. She had a determination about her to do whatever it took medically to get well, no matter what the risk.

Even as a child, whether in sports or activities, she had never been shy about taking a risk. Neither her father nor I had that nature, and we had to bite our lips and shut one eye at some of the things she did. One day she told me she would love to try to skydive, and I nearly fainted.

But this situation was different. I could tell she was a little annoyed at having to take an alternate route to what she felt God had called her to do. These tests were interfering with the timetable she had set to be at his work, for which she had prepared long and hard. At this point, she had not given up, but I could tell she felt disappointment. Yet the biopsy was the only and last thing that could identify the nature of the tumor.

William and I went to the surgery waiting room. The wait was unbearable—knowing the risk involved and what the results could reveal. The surgery took about five hours. We were allowed to go into the recovery room right after they took her in there. The doctor kept asking her to wiggle her toes, move her hand, look at his finger and follow it with her eyes, which she could do and we were thankful, because this meant the surgery had not paralyzed her. But I just wanted to cry when I saw her. She looked very weak. Most of her hair was gone. What was left they had twisted and pinned right on top of her head; from right above her ears down, it was shaved off. God gave me the strength to hold up in front of her.

Robyn held my hand but was not saying much, only yes or no responses to questions.

William's family, my family, and our friends were all calling to learn what we found out. We waited anxiously for a week. Robyn was flooded with cards and flowers and prayers.

When we were into the second week of waiting, I began asking why they would not tell us. At the end of the week, as I talked with one of the head nurses, sharing my anxious feelings, she said, "You don't know how hard it is for the doctor to tell you." She expressed how he had grown to love Robyn and that Robyn was so young.

My heart sank. I knew she was telling me the news was not good. I had already shared with the doctor that we were praying that the tumor would not be cancerous, and he said he was hoping it would be because it would respond better to treatment.

The next day, the doctor told us the biopsy had confirmed a tumor—called an astrocytoma—on the brain stem. On a scale of one to ten, with ten being most cancerous, the tumor was only about a two or three. This did not mean a whole lot to us yet, because we did not know what an astrocytoma was and the doctor did not offer an explanation. He did go on to say that surgery was not an option—they could not operate on the brain stem. I knew this was the worst news Robyn could hear, because all along she was thinking and telling her friends, "We'll do surgery and a treatment and then I can go on to my job in St. Louis."

William and I asked what to do since she could not have surgery. The doctor said after a few weeks we would do six weeks of radiation. We would have to make plans to have the radiation at Duke for a week at a time, but we could take Robyn home on weekends. He also said we had the option of having the treatments in Spartanburg, and he could tell doctors there how to administer it.

After the doctor left, we sat wondering what we would do now. My heart went out to Robyn because I knew she wanted a quick fix. She wanted to get on with her life and do what she had trained and studied and prepared herself for and what she felt God had called her to do. But here she was, trapped with an illness that would not let go, would not let her be the vivacious bundle of energy she had always been. Even as a child, three years younger than her brother, she would take him on and challenge him in any game or adventure her personality led her to pursue.

As friends and family began to contact us to learn of the prognosis after the biopsy, they expressed that same sense of wondering what was next—when was Robyn going to be Robyn again? I could not give up. I could not even, at this point, think of anything else but that God would intervene, that he had a purpose in this, and we were just to wait in prayer to see his will unfold.

We went home in a couple of days. Robyn was on a steroid, not feeling really good, not walking with good balance, and without an appetite. I tried to stay positive and issue encouragement every day. Someone gave her a book about fighting cancer and how not giving up was so important to healing. Her friends sent her cards, balloons, and letters, and many came to visit with her. These kept her going.

She had a week at home to rest before we were to take her back for the first radiation treatments. After some rain, we walked out on the porch and sat down together. Robyn was sharing some of her feelings and experiences at Duke. The cloudy, dark sky seemed to turn to a beautiful light blue, with a hint of sunlight, and a beautiful rainbow appeared in a never-ending arch. As we sat there and watched the paintbrush of God, I felt that he was speaking to us through that rainbow. Robyn wrote about it in her diary:

About two weeks after surgery, I have been very weak. I sleep most of the day and make myself get up to eat. It has been an awful, dependent feeling. Mom has to wash my hair and help give me a bath. Anyway, on September 22, Mom and I were sitting out on the front porch and a beautiful rainbow appeared. I have never seen one like it before. I was thinking it, but Mom said it—"This rainbow is a sign from God that you are going to be all right." I was so moved I couldn't say anything. Mom went in shortly after that, and I sat there and cried and thanked the Lord for his assurance during this time. Again, I felt a peace that only God can give. Amen!!!

CHAPTER 7

RADIATION

W E HAD TO decide with Robyn whether to go back to Duke for six weeks of treatment or have the treatment at Spartanburg Regional. I called the doctor in charge of radiation at Spartanburg Regional, who said she would call Duke and find out exactly how they wanted her to give the treatments. She asked me to bring Robyn to the hospital so she could talk with us. When we visited, she said they had never done a treatment like Duke was asking them to do but that she would communicate with Duke constantly and try to do it the way the orders were issued.

After we left, I asked Robyn what she wanted to do, and she said she would rather go to Duke. I didn't know how we were going to do it, but I wanted to go to Duke if Robyn had more confidence in their staff. William and I talked about it, and after looking at his calendar, he said he would miss work and go with her the first two weeks, and I could go for two weeks. Then we'd see about the last two weeks after that. Robyn, of course, had to be driven everywhere at this point because of the double vision and weakness. It was so hard for me to think about leaving school for two weeks at the beginning of the school year, but my heart knew we had to do it.

When I told my principal, he asked me if I had the accumulated days. I had more days than they would record because I was never absent, so I made plans to be gone. In the meantime, Mrs. Calkins, Robyn's second mother in Louisville, called and said she wanted to go with Robyn for two weeks to Duke and would take Jonathan with her. We couldn't believe she really meant this, but she was very insistent, so we discussed it with her and made plans for her to go the last two weeks.

William took Robyn up to Duke a few days before the treatments started for the assimilation, which would pinpoint the radiation and set up how the treatments would be given. It was tiring and uncomfortable for Robyn because of the measuring, making the apparatus, and putting her on the table and adjusting, and it was difficult for William to observe. Robyn, however, still showed that spirit of hope and determination to pursue whatever it took to help her heal.

When the treatments started, we soon worked out a routine. Robyn had to be at the hospital by eight in the morning and wait in the waiting room until she was called. We usually just ate something in the room at the motel since this was so early. The treatment would take an hour to an hour and a half. We would go back to the motel so she could lie down because she was so washed-out and weak after the treatment. When I was there with her at Duke, I would then go to a nearby park with a walking trail and a little pond—a very beautiful and peaceful setting. I enjoyed a walk there, often stopping along the way to sit on a bench and talk with God. I was praying for complete healing and would not entertain any thought of losing my daughter.

Robyn wrote about the first day of radiation in her diary:

It didn't hurt at all! In the evening, my ears have started to bother me. I'll ask the doctor about it Wednesday. I will see the doctor then. I continue to feel a peace that God is in control of this whole situation. He is going to get rid of this tumor. The machine clicks as the radiation goes in—as it is clicking, I say to myself, *Kill that tumor.* I also continue to ask God for assurances along the way. He has provided! The daily devotional my youth gave me said the following for today, "O Lord, I believe you are with me, helping me, and I believe in time of sorrow, you will strengthen me." AMEN!! For the first day of treatment, I thought this was very appropriate. Thanks, Lord. I can't describe the feeling of assurance when I read this. Also, today I read an article in *Reader's Digest* about brain tumors. It said tumors that are inoperable could now be treated with radiation. Ten years ago this wasn't possible. I feel very fortunate and even more assured by reading this. God is going to see me through this "obstacle."

We had a little two-door Honda at this time. It was good on mileage, but small for long trips to Duke with someone who wasn't feeling well, and Robyn was nearly six feet tall; she couldn't stretch out and be comfortable. So I was thinking we would have to get a van when Robyn got better. I could imagine her as her vivacious self again, telling everyone how God had led her through this and healed her.

After William stayed with her for the first two weeks, I made plans for a substitute for the next two weeks. I took work with me to Duke, and when I came home with Robyn on the weekends, the substitute and I talked about how things were going with my students. I worked on things for school when I wasn't doing something for Robyn or transporting her from the hotel to the hospital. We ate a light lunch and looked around at some of the stores if she felt like it and then went back to the motel. Robyn did not have much appetite, so we tried to pick different places to encourage her to eat.

Every day when we went for treatment, we saw many of the same people in the waiting room. We came to know them very well. One lady had an astrocytoma in her leg, and one older man had a brain tumor also. We shared feelings of concern, uncertainty, and love for those we were there for, and most important, an assurance of God's care. Robyn was one of the youngest patients. When I had opportunity to talk about her, people were so caring and complimentary about what she had accomplished so far in her life and her work in the future at the orphanage.

In December, we went back to Southern Seminary for Robyn to receive her degree. She was wearing glasses with the right side smoked in, and she was quite thin. We asked one of her best friends to walk across the stage with her because she was unstable, and her friend was proud to do this. It happened that this particular friend had many health problems and had taken a slower, lighter load of studies at the seminary. She had said that Robyn was her crutch, her encourager, and her supporter, the only one who could help her when she got depressed and felt like she could not go on.

It was a beautiful ceremony and celebration. Everyone was so thrilled Robyn could be there, and she was so thankful she could be there, although she did not feel well. I was so proud of her and was praying that she was going to be able to use her training in the future for God's glory. I just wanted to bawl when she tried to walk across the stage.

After the first week that I was with her at Duke, we were eating lunch at a unique little restaurant we had found off the beaten path. When we went in the restaurant, there were some *USA Today* newspapers for anyone who wanted to pick one up. Because I had not read the paper since we had been at Duke, I decided to take one. I was thumbing through it while we waited for our food, and a page with an article on brain tumors caught my eye.

The article named three brain tumors that were terminal; the first one on the list was astrocytoma. I scanned down the page and read about the symptoms. Once the diagnosis was made, the article said, life expectancy was three to nine months.

My appetite started to fade. I couldn't believe what I was reading. I felt like my face had flushed. I quietly slipped the paper down off the table and tried not to show any emotion. I was in shock. I wanted to just get up and run. Here was Robyn, sitting right in front of me, eyeball to eyeball, looking weak and drained. This was the first time I had read, or been told, or faced the fact that Robyn's cancer could be terminal. The doctors at Duke had never said this. My faith was weak, but I would not even entertain the idea of losing her.

As the waitress placed our lunch in front of us, I tried to regain my composure. I asked God for strength and put what I had just read in the back of my mind. I started a conversation with Robyn. Robyn had always been so attractive and stately; the nurses at Duke said she looked like a model. Now she was losing weight each day, her hair was so thin, and sometimes she wore a patch on one eye. Even without the patch, it was noticeable that her eye was turning toward her nose. It really hurt me to look at her. Also, her voice was not the same.

I tried to engage her in conversation, but it was hard for me to think of something to ignite her interest. The newspaper article had thrown cold water all over me. We attempted to finish our meal together and then went back to the motel for Robyn to lie down and rest. I felt I needed to take a little walk so I could talk with God.

I realized I wasn't telling God anything he didn't know or that wasn't in his master plan, but I felt he needed to know what I had just found out, and I needed to put in another special request to him. Every day I talked to him constantly, as were all of Robyn's friends from two colleges and the seminary she had attended, every church that had been informed about her, and the orphanage where she was going to work. I remembered that one of her friends called me one day and said, "Martha, I don't know of any denomination that is not praying for Robyn. I even have some Catholic neighbors who called and said, 'We lit a candle and said a prayer for Robyn.'" I thought of a chorus that fit so well: "When I walk, I walk with Jesus, when I talk, I talk with Jesus, when I sing, I sing of Jesus, for he's with me all the way."

When we were home on weekends, Robyn was constantly on the phone with her friends or they were at the house. Todd took her to a ball game one night at Furman. Robyn had played basketball and loved it, and she loved the excitement of being at the game. I cautioned Todd to stay right by her side, as she was so weak.

Robyn wrote this poem while we were at Duke:

> I love babies that burp,
> Rainbows in the sky and birds that chirp,
> I love you too!
> I love friends that laugh, talking on the phone,
> And having a blast and
> I love you too!
> I love the life that God gives,
> The love that he shows,
> And the miracle of friends and family,
> And I love you too!
> I love going to church,
> Singing the hymns and being with friends, and I love you
> too!
> I love experiencing God,
> Knowing he's close
> And watching me the most, caring for me,
> And I love you too!!
> I love Raggedy Ann and Andy,
> Scooby Doo and vanilla milkshakes
> And I love you too!

Mrs. Calkins and Jonathan took Robyn to Duke for the last two weeks of her treatments. Mrs. Calkins was determined to do this and, having faith that Robyn would beat this trauma in her life, I agreed to let her help out in this way. William and I were so grateful not to have to lose more time at our jobs. We talked with Robyn every day by phone. I tried to pray harder, and everyone knew I was praying. We bought a book about cancer that was highly recommended; the main thought was that half the battle of winning was not to give up, that attitude is so important. I read the book aloud to Robyn when she felt so weak and her eye was bothering her.

RADIATION

When she came home, two members of William's Sunday school class came to lay hands on her and anoint her with oil and pray. When she felt like it, we would go out for a while. For Christmas I bought her a beautiful suede skirt and top. However, we all were somewhat depressed because we remembered the live wire she had always been. Now she had lost most of her hair, was so thin, talked differently, and wore glasses with one lens shaded in so she would not see double.

DEAR ROBYN. I LOVE YOU. VERY
MUCH I HOPE YOU GET WELL
SOON. CLARA IS FINE. FOR YOU
AND ME I LOVE YOU. VERY
MUCH. BECAUSE (CAUSE) PEOPLE
LOVE AND LIKE PEOPLE FOREVER
AND EVER AND EVER AND EVER
AND EVER AND EVER AND EVER
BUT YOU. KNOW ROBYN YOU
SHOULD. GET WELL. SOON.
                LOVE, JONATHAN

RADIATION

Southern Seminary
Graduation

Robyn with a friend at Seminary

Some of Robyn's relatives.

Friends at Southern

RADIATION

December Graduation

December Graduation

RADIATION

A note from a friend Robyn- about Graduation. We went through a lot.

You're someone very special,
So this comes
with pride and love
To wish you all the happy things
You're so deserving of,
To thank you for the happiness
You always give away
And to tell you that
you're loved much more
Than words could ever say.

We are so proud of you finishing your
MSW at Southern. Only with God's help could we
have helped you accomplish this. Our constant
prayer has been that He will lead you and we
just have to trust Him in faith knowing that
He takes care of you. What a priviledge and
pleasure and Christian joy we have had in caring
for and watching you grow in your love for the
Lord. We are excited for you and Praise God and
give Him the Glory for every gain of growth

Robyn,

We went through a whole lot
to get this degree, didn't we?!
I'm so glad (especially the last
year) that we were friends
through it, because you taught
me a lot about what is and
isn't important. I have great
respect for you, and I was
so proud to see you walk
across that stage today.

RADIATION

DEAR ROBYN,
        I MISS YOU! I LOVE YOU! HOW
ARE YOU DOING? AT NIGHT I SAY THAT
YOU GET BETTER SOON. MOMMY SAID
WE WILL COME TO SEE YOU, AS SOON
AS KIMMIE HAS THE BABY. I LIKE
SCHOOL NOW. I MADE A FRIEND NAMED
DAVID. ANGELA BABYSITTS ME. NOW.
 HOPE WE GET TO SEE YOU SOON.
I LOVE YOU!!!!!!!!!!!!!!!!!!!
JONATHAN

CONGRATULATIONS!

Because you have attained a scholastic ranking
within the top 20% of your class, you have
met the initial requirement for membership
in The Gamma Beta Phi Society,
a national collegiate honor
and service organization.

Additional information about Gamma Beta Phi may
be obtained at a meeting for prospective
members, Monday, March 12, at 5 p.m.
in Room 212 of Watkins Teaching Center.
If you are unable to attend this meeting,
contact Mr. or Mrs. Hoyte
in Rooms 115 or 117.

CHAPTER 8

REALITY

I RETURNED TO teaching my class with the burden of Robyn's health ever present on my mind. I prayed that God would give me strength to teach little children and be the mother I needed to be at this time. I really did not want to go back to school; I wanted to be with Robyn. However, the bills were pages long by this time, and I knew we were going to need both my salary and William's to get through all this. I just had to trust God and put Robyn in his hands.

Not long after I had returned to school, my principal called me out of class and said, "Mrs. Axmann, the district has decided to deduct your pay for the two weeks you were out. There is a phrase in the handbook stating accumulated days can't be used for the sickness of a relative."

Now this was never mentioned when I told him I had the accumulated days. My principal had agreed that if I had the days, I could go to Duke to be with Robyn. I could not believe what I was hearing. I had talked with him in detail before I left.

My mental and emotional state was too tired at this time to conceive of what they were thinking. The faculty at my school couldn't believe it. Even the district superintendent's secretary couldn't believe it, and she expressed her opinion about it to her boss. I wrote the superintendent a letter, expressing that whether it was called emotional illness, physical illness, or mental illness; any one of those would apply to what I was going through due to the illness of my daughter. I had taught and been at school on days that my heart wanted to be with her, but I had stayed true to my contract. I wanted the district to know how disappointed I was, along with the faculty at my school and other friends in the district.

When I received my check, the pay had been taken out.

Robyn completed the radiation treatments and was home for several weeks now, trying to recover and gain strength back after the radiation. She was very weak, had very little appetite, and was on steroids. I would come home from teaching and try to get her out for a ride or a walk. It was so painful for me to look at her and see how this terrible illness had engulfed her physical appearance and affected her vivacious personality. I tried not to let my depressed feelings show.

Time moved slowly some days and far too quickly on others. I remember in the latter part of January, as Robyn and I were slowly walking through a store, Robyn said, "Mom, I need some money to buy valentines." I almost cried—she wanted to send valentines to all her friends and some of the children she had worked with in Louisville at Spring Meadows Children's Home and at the church where she was youth director. This was such a lesson to me and showed the true character of who Robyn was inside. She was so sick and weak and did not know what the future held, but she was still concerned and loved all her friends and wanted them to know it. So we bought valentines for her seminary friends typical of their personalities and some children's valentines with cute messages for the children.

Robyn loved her college roommate at Anderson University like a sister. Stacy had called and wanted Robyn to be the maid of honor in her wedding. She had put off the wedding until Robyn finished her radiation; she said she was not going to have the wedding without her. Robyn agreed to do it, although she was very weak.

I took Robyn for her dress fitting and again witnessed such an emotional down. Robyn had lost so much weight that it was hard for the seamstress to make the dress look right on her. She was also still wearing glasses with one lens smoked so she would not see double images. Through all these difficulties, she was determined to be there for Stacy.

Stacy coveted Robyn's opinion and advice. She and Robyn had discussed in detail the plans for the wedding and how it was to be carried out. The day of the wedding, she called Robyn crying about things not being ready, and Robyn spent a lot of time encouraging her to continue her plans.

Todd had taken Robyn to the rehearsal dinner, and we all were with her at the wedding. We helped Robyn get ready and went early so Robyn could help if needed. The church was not decorated yet, and Stacy's brother was running around sticking magnolia leaves and a candle in each window. Finally things came together, and the wedding was pretty. Stacy looked the best I had ever seen her, and Robyn looked pretty also. Most young people would not have wanted to be seen in public with what she was going through, but Robyn was determined to be there for Stacy, since they loved each other so much.

Robyn's doctor said the MRI right after the six weeks of radiation looked better. He had a difficult time identifying any abnormal brain cells. I wrote in my prayer journal, "Praise the Lord." We were to return in about six weeks.

William took her back since I had missed so many days of teaching. When they came home, they both had such depressed looks that I knew they had not received good news. Robyn could hardly talk about it and looked like she would fall over if I touched her. I could tell she just wanted to rest and give all this to the Lord.

William said to me, "Martha, it's not good." He said the doctor was puzzled that her symptoms were not any better after she had such a good MRI previously. We discussed this for a time after we got Robyn to bed. All he was telling me was what I did not want to hear. I just couldn't give in to the idea of losing Robyn. I kept thinking and praying for a miracle. That was a long, hard, tearful night.

In a sermon, our pastor talked about the faith of Shadrach, Meshach, and Abednego, who said their God would protect their lives but, even if he didn't, they would still worship him. Dr. Walker said, "Don't measure your faith by the answers—trust in God, but if the answers are not what you ask for, it doesn't mean you have not the faith."

All this time, the administration at the children's home in St. Louis was telling Robyn that time did not matter; they were holding the job for her whenever she was able to come. They wanted her on staff so very much. Ramona, her roommate in St. Louis, continued living alone in their apartment, and since this was expensive for her we continued to send her Robyn's share of the rent.

Toward the end of January, one of the doctors from Duke called Robyn and asked her how she was doing. She described some of her problems to him—difficulty swallowing, unstable when walking, and weakness. He did not offer encouragement. He said there was nerve damage. She told him they were still holding her job in St. Louis and asked when he thought she could go. He expressed that she should not even think about going to St. Louis; he did not know if she would ever be able to go.

This was just like setting a bomb off in her face. All hope was blown out from under her. Her hope to do what she had lived for, planned for, gone to school for, and prepared for was blown away. So qualified, prepared, and ready to give her talents back to the Lord, so much to offer, and here was this wall—her physical body that would not allow her to give of herself.

In my Bible reading, I read Luke 17:11–19, which tells about the healing of the lepers, and John 15:7, which says, "If you remain in me and my words remain in you, ask whatever you wish, and it will be given you." I also read Luke 18:1–8, the story Jesus used to teach his followers that we should always pray and never lose hope. I thanked God for that verse, our hope in him.

I think after the doctor did not give her any encouragement about returning to St. Louis, Robyn started turning over in her mind that maybe she could do a little something in Spartanburg. She mentioned this to me, and I suggested she go and talk with a respected minister in our church who was also a counselor. She did this, and he advised her, more or less, to rest and do everything she could to gain back her physical strength first. She really was not up to any kind of social work or church work at this time, but she would not give up to that.

A young man from Anderson whom I had taught wrote this letter to her:

> Dear Robyn,
>
> Although I have never met you, I feel that I know you. Your dedication and commitment to Christ have impressed me and inspired me.
>
> Daily, I pray that God will deliver you, yet I praise him for the positive influence your struggle has had on my life. I admire you for your courage and determination and your Christ-centered life.
>
> Although I'm sure you don't realize it, you have helped me through a very crucial phase in my Christian development. I had reached this juncture, which every Christian eventually arrives at, where I had to decide the scope of my dedication. Would I "live Christ" as you have done (loving him, serving him, praising him, giving him my all) or would I just put Christ aside as if he were a ticket I would put in my wallet, which I would use for admission into heaven?
>
> Hearing about your unyielding faith and hope had an integral part in my decision to serve Christ with my life.
>
> For helping me reach this decision, I cannot thank you enough.
>
> In closing, I leave to you a few thoughts from a "loose translation" of Lamentations 3:22–33: "Because of the Lord's great love, we are not consumed, O for his compassions never fail. They are new every morning, great is your faithfulness." I

say to myself, "The Lord is my portion; Therefore, I will wait for him." The Lord is good to those whose hope is in him, to the one who seeks him. It is good to wait quietly for the salvation of the Lord. It is good for a woman to bear the yoke while she is young. For you will not be cast off by the Lord forever; though he brings grief, he will show compassion, so great is his unfailing love. For he does not willingly bring affliction or grief to his children.

Robyn, I pray for you as you struggle with an impossible decision. May God bless you and watch over you.

Your brother in Christ,

Brian

What an encouragement this letter was to all of us!

On February 1 we all went to a fancy restaurant in Greenville to celebrate Robyn's birthday. The waiters came out and sang to her. It was really all the entertainment she had strength for at the time. She wrote in her diary, "I only went out with Mom and Dad and my brother for my birthday and missed the usual 'blast' I have always had with my friends."

Birthdays were a time of big celebration for Robyn. One year, when I was teaching in Anderson, on my birthday she sent a clown to school with balloons and music. When she was in the seminary, there was a party at the home of the Calkins family, with food, games, and costumes. So it seemed our little dining-out party was not enough for her. (Just wait till I get to heaven and let her know about this!)

About the end of February, Dr. Diana Garland, one of Robyn's seminary professors, took a tape recorder to class, and each student who wanted to went into a separate room alone and talked on tape to Robyn. Each message was so unique and special. Some students were uncertain about what to say to someone who had been the life of the campus and so quickly diagnosed with a terminal illness. Many said something like, "I don't know how to put into words how we miss you and how sad we are about what you are going through." I thought one friend summed up everyone's thoughts so well. She said, "Robyn, I'm just going to sing a song to you that says what we feel." She sang the song by Jim Gilbert, adapting the lyrics slightly: "We love you with the love of the Lord, we love you with the love of the Lord. And we see in you the glory of our King, and we love you with the love of the Lord!"

CHAPTER 9

At the Finish Line

ALWAYS IN FEBRUARY, Robyn's grandparents in Anderson went to the beach to visit with my husband's brother and his wife. When we were over at their house on a Sunday eating lunch, William's mom casually mentioned that they were going and said that if Robyn felt like it, she could go with them. After Robyn thought for a few minutes, she said, "I'll think I'll go."

I was shocked. In the first place, I knew Robyn was not up to a trip to Florida. In the second place, I knew William's mom and dad. As much as I loved them, I knew that if Robyn had a problem they would not interrupt their vacation to bring her home. In the third place, Robyn was at a place physically where she needed to be within driving distance of her doctors.

Her grandparents were shocked but did not want to say, "No, you'd better not go" after they had issued the invitation. I think they had invited her just to be nice. I did not want to confront her in front of them about this, and I thought, *Well, maybe I'm being too protective of her.* They insisted she go.

We took her to their house late in the afternoon for them to leave early the next morning. My heart was breaking to see her go. They did not have an extra bedroom, so she had to sleep on the couch that night. The trip wore her out. She had to lie down most of the way. I talked to her the first day, and it seemed a little harder to understand her. The next day, her grandmother called and said Robyn couldn't talk; she had lost her voice. I immediately said, "Robyn needs to come home." But her grandmother never agreed.

The following day, her grandmother said Robyn wasn't feeling well and still could not talk. Again, I asked her to bring Robyn home. She seemed to think everything would be all right. They finally brought her home one day earlier than they had planned. My son met them in Anderson and brought Robyn on to Spartanburg. When she got out of the car, I could not believe how bad she looked and how weak she was. She could not utter a word.

I called her doctor at Duke that night and he said to take her on to the hospital in Spartanburg, that she was not able to make the trip to Duke. He said he would keep in touch with the doctor in Spartanburg and give his opinion. We called a neurologist in Spartanburg, although he had never seen her, and I told him Robyn needed to go to the hospital that night. He said no; he would not admit her and to call him in the morning. I insisted, and he asked me to put Robyn on the phone. I told him she could not talk. He said, "Let me hear her." I was a basket case by this time. Robyn tried to utter some sounds but could not make a word come out. She handed me the phone but the doctor still said, "Just bring her in the morning."

It was a horrible night. Robyn wasn't breathing well either. She was so weak as we went into the emergency room the next morning, we carried practically all her weight. It was late afternoon before we got her in a room. In a few hours, she needed a tracheotomy so she could breathe. This was so alarming to all of us and to her, a hole in her throat, and she was looking weaker and weaker. When I looked at her, I tried not to let on and tried to stay cheerful for her as much as possible.

At this time, she was not talking, just writing notes on a notepad. She did not hear well either, and we had already had tubes put in to help that. She couldn't tell us when she needed to go to the bathroom; she would just point. Sometimes she was able to walk to the bathroom with help, and sometimes she used the bedpan because she was so weak.

I was trying to teach as much as I could and then go to the hospital after school. William was at the hospital as much as he could be, before and after work. I wanted to take Robyn back to Duke, but she was so weak we did not think she could make the trip.

I was disappointed with the doctor in Spartanburg. I asked Robyn if she would rather go to Duke and she said yes. When the doctor in Spartanburg finally did admit her on the morning we took her in, he more or less lectured William and me about Duke. He said Robyn was not going to live and we might as well face it and he couldn't get over that we had not been told that at Duke.

Of course, we all were aware of what was going on, and we knew how sick Robyn was, and I did not need to hear all of this with what we were going through at this time. I appreciated the care and concern we had been given at Duke. This was the first time this doctor in Spartanburg had seen her and the first time he had met us. It was just all so very hard.

I felt like my hands were tied. I knew Robyn wanted to go back to Duke, but she was not physically able. I had endured the pain of slowly seeing her regress physically and emotionally. She had so much to give but now was so limited in every way. I just hurt for her, and now we had to deal with an inconsiderate, insensitive doctor. He wasn't telling us anything we did not know or hadn't been living with for the past several months. For my state of mind and for Robyn's sake, I felt that the less we saw of him the better for everyone. Since Robyn was so weak and sick at this time, we had to stay in Spartanburg.

Robyn's friends came constantly to the hospital in Spartanburg, showing their love for her. The staff there told me they were giving her the largest room in the hospital because she had so many friends. William's parents came later that week. His mother walked down the hall with me, and she said, "Martha, don't give up. She is going to live. I just know God is going to heal her." I told her I had never given up. I felt the same way.

One day, right after I walked into Robyn's room, she wrote me a note saying all that was on TV were food commercials and it looked so good. I wanted to cry for her. She could not swallow.

Her roommate from the seminary, Deena, came. She wrote Robyn notes that said, "We are not going to let you die. We are all praying." Another seminary friend asked me if he could just talk to her by himself. He stayed so long that I walked back into the room just to check on her. He was telling her what she meant to him and how much he thought of her and how she had inspired so many. He went on and on, even when I walked back into the room.

I had a sister who lived close by who stayed with Robyn while I was at school. On the morning of March 11, she called me at school and told me to come immediately. One of the doctors had been in and was talking to Robyn about putting a feeding tube in and maybe we could bring her home and he would teach me how to use it at home. He said Robyn acted like she knew what he was talking about and understood. And then, all of a sudden, she didn't respond.

The guidance counselor took my class, and I drove to the hospital as quickly as I could. William was already there, and two friends from Anderson were standing outside the room. When I walked in the room, I felt like God had his chariot parked outside the door and had come for her. She was still breathing but her eyes were glazed. William stood on one side of the bed, holding her hand, while I was on the other. I told her I loved her and tried to get a response, but she just peacefully crossed the finish line into God's arms.

Robyn lived twenty-nine and a half weeks from the day she was diagnosed. My husband wrote in his notes:

We prayed it would not be a brain tumor but—
We prayed it would not be malignant but—
We prayed it would not be inoperable but—
We prayed that she would live but—

A friend asked, "Aren't you mad at God?" Even one of her seminary professors said, "I can't understand why she was taken."

Jesus never promised life would be fair or that it would be easy. He did promise to be with us all the time, and I feel he has been.

One night, when William was holding me and was telling me good-night, he said, "And to think, Robyn never got to experience the love and joy of a marriage like we have and the pleasure of having her own children." The ocean of tears and emotions I was feeling would not allow a verbal response. William's love for me and for Robyn was so evident and stabilizing. I just wanted to say "Thank you, God, for being with us." I thought of a line from a Michael W. Smith song, "Draw me close to you. Never let me go."

CHAPTER 10

CELEBRATION OF LIFE

NOW I WAS faced with planning the funeral of my only daughter. I tried to think through what she would want and things she had told me.

From time to time, Robyn would tell me how special her wedding was going to be. As we would be shopping (something she and I both loved to do), she would say, "Mom, I want this at my wedding." Every time she told me something else she wanted at her wedding, I cringed because, as wonderful as my husband was and as extraordinary a provider as he had been for us through the years, he might not be willing to spend the money needed for an extravagant wedding like I knew Robyn wanted. She had dated several different young men we all liked, but she had her eye set on her goal and she was determined to complete it. One young man at Anderson College was crazy about her, but I don't think she even entertained the idea of marriage at that time in her life.

One day Robyn had told me she wanted a bell choir at her wedding. I thought to myself, *Robyn, I don't even know where there is a bell choir, and if I did know of one, I wonder what the tab for that would be, plus the orchestra and soloist you want.* But when Robyn set her mind to what she wanted to achieve or accomplish, she drove herself to do it, and maybe I did have some of that drive myself. I wanted a bell choir for the funeral. I asked a group from Anderson First Baptist to come, and they did.

I asked Dr. Jim Whitlow, vice president of Anderson College, and Rev. Sandy Kidd, the campus pastor, to lead the service along with Dr. Diana Garland, associate professor of social work at Southern Seminary, and Rev. Bob Morgan, from my church in Spartanburg. A mother of one of Robyn's best friends from Anderson was in the bell choir that came from Anderson.

As Rev. Morgan opened the service, he said, "We will make this a worship service, as I feel this is what Robyn would desire. We know the One who said, 'Whosoever liveth and believeth in me shall never die.' We come to celebrate eternal life. To God be the glory."

Rev. Kidd read Psalm 121, Joel 2:28, Jeremiah 33, and Isaiah 41:8–10, some of Robyn's favorite scriptures.

Over several days, I contacted many who had the privilege of teaching Robyn. Several of them spoke at the service, and their words were dear to our hearts:

Her basketball coach spoke of Robyn as a team leader, an encourager, a teachable person, and one who would give it her all.

On of Robyn's English teachers said Robyn was bright and creative, with a particular ability to take a stand among her peers about her faith in her Savior, Jesus Christ, and how rare that ability was.

One of Robyn's teachers at Anderson College said Robyn had a great love of life and energy and tremendous leadership ability, and that she represented the best part of Anderson College. Another faculty member said Robyn was "one of the coolest students we ever had. She had it together. She was the kind of student you wanted to have in your class."

A student from Anderson said, "I came with my Dad to visit the college and Robyn took us around campus. She was so friendly even to me, a stranger. She was a deciding factor in my coming to Anderson College. The neatest thing about her was the communication did not stop at that point; she stayed in contact with me. She wrote me letters of encouragement, and when I graduated [from high school] I received a package from her with a notepad printed with my name on it and the Anderson College emblem. This made me feel so special."

The chaplain at Anderson College said, "Robyn's service [as president of campus ministries] at Anderson College put me in daily contact with her as her chaplain. She would come into my office with great joy—wonderful smile, relaxed attitude; her spirit and her commitment to Christ were so impressive. Robyn touched a very deep part of my soul."

Then the bell choir played.

Dr. Whitlow read 1 Corinthians 13 and shared the following words:

Paul tells us the three characteristics of Christians are faith, hope, and love—these were evident in Robyn's life. Faith was so evident in her life; she was so joyful with those around her. Her summers were spent as a youth director in churches, a summer missionary to Bermuda, a camp counselor, and in many other forms of Christian service. Her faith was real. She uplifted those around her. She lived by her faith and died in the Lord. She had a life filled with hope.

Robyn loved to laugh. When Robyn was finishing her degree, she was at my office and I asked her what kind of job she wanted. She said, "I want your job. I want to be vice president, sit behind a desk, and tell other people what to do!" Robyn put hope into life—the way she walked, talked, and the very way she shook your hand or told you a story.

She was a gentle, loving person. She loved her friends and family in a special way. What seemed to give her the most delight were her close friends. Her face would light up when she told about her family. One of the greatest expressions of her love was seen in her love for children. I have a picture in my mind of Robyn in a park in Bermuda, on a college mission trip, with twenty or thirty children all around her, on her lap, on her back, as she told them stories about little things. Her love was a special love that reached to everyone.

John 14:1–6; Matthew 6:30; Matthew 11:28; Romans 8:28 were read, and then Dr. Garland's letter was read by Dr. Morgan since she was sick and could not come the day of the service.

> I and the faculty and students of the Southern Baptist Theological Seminary grieve the loss of our dear sister, Robyn Axmann. She has ministered in the name of Jesus to countless young people, both as a church youth director and as a professional social worker in our Baptist Children's Home in Kentucky. Robyn lived out Jesus' command to welcome children into the kingdom. She used her own life in words, hugs, and laughter to reach out to young people in crisis in the name of Jesus. Robyn channeled her love through skillful professional practice in ways that changed lives. She knew the meaning of friendship and gave of herself for her friends. She found humor and joy even in the midst of the stressful crush of all the responsibilities she carried.
>
> Burdens were lighter and troubles less stressful when I could share them with Robyn. I grieve that her life was so short because she stood on the brink of a whole new phase in her ministry and because I will miss the hope and promise I felt in her presence. But I also rejoice in the gift she has been to me and to her other friends here and to the children and youth she loved and ministered to.
>
> It has been said whether life is long or short, its completeness depends on what it was lived for. Robyn's life, though short, was full. She lived for others. She made God more real to those who knew her through her touch and care. Robyn's presence will long be felt in this place and in the lives of her friends who are now scattered to the four corners of the world in ministry. I thank God for Robyn Axmann.

Rev. Morgan also spoke:

> I want you to hear a letter that was sent to Robyn from a young person in Anderson who had never met her personally, but Robyn had influenced him. He knew of her condition and commitment to the Lord through friends. [Brian's letter, printed in chapter 8, was read.]

In closing, I want to read Lamentations 3:22–33. [The passage ends, "Though he brings grief, he will show compassion, so great is his unfailing love. For he does not willingly bring affliction or grief to the children of men."]

Why? When there are so many individuals who seemingly could not make a contribution to the betterment of the world—why does God take one who had dedicated her life to the betterment of mankind?

These are the questions in our heart. Questions we all have to ask: What will I do for Jesus Christ? If I walk away from this service without a new commitment to Jesus Christ, or without assuming a task for him or walk in his steps—perhaps it is I who is dead.

The service concluded with one of Robyn's favorite songs, "The Wind Beneath My Wings." God truly was the wind beneath her wings!

At the graveside, Dr. Whitlow and Rev. Kidd read Scripture and we listened to another one of Robyn's favorite songs, "I Have Friends in High Places," by Larnelle Harris. Many, many of her friends had come from all over and were standing around the family in a circle. As the song was sung, I reached out and held the hand of the one closest to me.

On Robyn's headstone, I put Proverbs 3:5–6: "Trust in the Lord with all thine heart; and lean not unto thine own understanding. In all thy ways acknowledge Him, and He shall direct thy paths. KJV

SHE WON THE RACE

This was the Christmas Card I sent to friends after her death.

Eph 1:16

Martha, William & Todd

Highland Park First Baptist Church
7321 Billtown Road
Louisville, Kentucky 40299
231-3917/231-3918

Dr. Jerry Browning
Pastor

Mr. & Mrs. William Axman
308 Woodgrove Trace
Spartanburg, South Carolina
29501

Dear Mr. & Mrs. Axman,

My name is Jerry Browning. I am pastor of the Highland Park First Baptist Church here in Louisville. On behalf of our congregation I want to let you know that we have placed a plaque with Robyn's name on one of the front pews in our sanctuary in honor of her memory.

Although she has gone on to be with the Lord, her influence lives on in the lives of all the people she has touched. Thank you again for sharing her with us.

Yours in Christ,

Jerry Browning

Reaching and Growing Together

Picture of Becky, one of the youth that was in the church where Robyn was youth director. She wrote, "The Best Youth Director Ever-Love, Becky."

IN LOVING MEMORY OF
ROBYN AXMANN
OUR MINISTER OF YOUTH
FROM JUNE 26, 1988 TO APRIL 15, 1990

Church in Louisville where she was Youth director.

CELEBRATION OF LIFE

Her life was like a song –
A melody of perfect harmony
bringing joy to those it touched.

Because of her love of God,
Her love of people, and
Her love of music,

We dedicate this new Baptist Hymnal
to the glory of God
and in memory of
Robyn Axmann.

This was Mountain Creek Baptist Church when she was a youth in High School and I was the choir director.

SHE WON THE RACE

Jonathan Calkins
10/3/96
Scott

When I was 6 months old, I moved from Seffner (near Tampa) to Goshen (near Louisville, Kentucky). From a seminary school, I got a babysitter, who was absolutely wonderful, by the name of Robyn Axmann. Over the years, Robyn, and her best friend, Deena, became nearly as close to me as a part of the family. Robyn was about 6 ft tall, with the best brown sparkly eyes, and a wonderful laugh. She used to swing me under her leg, and, in Mom's fake vegetable basket, she would stick up the carrots and spread out the roots. Once Mom hid them, and of course I told Robyn where they were. When I was 3, Mom told me that Robyn was very sick and that we needed to go to the Carolinas to help her. In fact, Robyn had cancer of the brain. Th Axmanns lived in Spartanburg, South Carolina, and for a few terrible months, Robyn was in the hospital at Duke University, Durham, North Carolina. I used to write letters on the computer to her in the hospital...oh. Then one night, March 11, 1991, Mon came back from the hospital with tears running down her cheeks Robyn, the babysitter who was more than a babysitter, the youn woman who was part of the family, the tall black-haired person who had cared and loved for me for nearly 4 years, was dead. I cried for a long time, actually, I am making myself cry right now. She died 8 days before my 4th birthday. One day in April of '91, came home from Sunday School happily telling my parents that Robyn would arise from the dead like Jesus did. My mom explained it to me, and I went down in the dumps nearly until the time we moved to Jacksonville, in late April. Deena bought me a book called Someone I Love Died, which helped some. I sometimes wish Robyn was still alive, but then I think of how happy she is in heaven.

Dear Mr. & Mrs. Axmann,   10-16-90

I always tell Robyn when I write her or call her to tell you hello. I decided I wanted to write you for myself!

Both of you have been in my thoughts and prayers since this crisis started. I know how upset I've been as Robyn's friend. I know you feel it ten times more as her parents. I have been so impressed with Robyn's positive outlook and yours too. I'm glad she has such a great family!

I look forward to the day Robyn can start work here. No one has forgotten her at the children's home. People always tell me they're praying for her and ask me how she's doing. Each of us has a mail slot — Robyn's name is on one. They really are committed to Robyn working there.

I have appreciated you sending rent for the apartment. I know that's a financial hardship. I wish that I could help more. Remember, whatever you want me to do concerning the apartment is what I want. I feel that Robyn is going to be here soon, but please let me know if you need me to make other arrangements.

I'm praying for you and Robyn daily.

Love,
Ramona

CELEBRATION OF LIFE

DUKE UNIVERSITY MEDICAL CENTER

Division of Neurology

March 21, 1991

Mr. William Axmann
308 Woodgrove Trace
Spartanburg, South Carolina 29301

Dear Mr. Axmann:

We were all very saddened to learn of Robyn's death. She clearly had a worse tumor than the original histology indicated, and I'm surprised and extremely disappointed that things didn't go better. She clearly was a wonderful person and had a fine family, and our thoughts and prayers go out to you.

We intend to and will conquer this disease someday. We have a very active research program and there are a number of people here who put a great deal of effort into understanding this terrible disease. I'd like to keep you informed of our progress over the years in hopes that that progress will somehow help your own personal wounds heal.

Thank you very much for taking the time to write me a letter. I'll inform Drs. Cook and Halperin.

All best wishes.

Sincerely,

S. Clifford Schold, Jr., M. D.
Professor of Neurology

SCS:tjh

Dear Mr. and Mrs. Axmann and Todd,

Please know that my thoughts and prayers continue to be with you all and the other members of your family.

The memorial service at Seminary was very special. I was glad that I could take off work to go. It was held in the chapel in the new building. People were standing along the walls because the pews were full.

Gloria mentioned in her time to share at the memorial that she and Jon Rainbow had decided that, "Heaven is a lot more fun now that Robyn is there." That made me smile

RACING ON

So many times I had heard Robyn tell her friends,
"Go for it!"
First Corinthians 15:58 tells me to give fully to the work of the
Lord—my labor is not in vain.
Now I could hear Robyn telling me, "Go for it, Mom."
I must look for opportunities and "Go for it for the Lord."
This is what we are left here to do. I know that, Robyn.

CHAPTER 11

"WRITE IT DOWN"

AFTER A FEW weeks, William, Todd, and I returned to St. Louis to get Robyn's things. We drove William's small Mazda truck, and we borrowed a truck from my brother-in-law because we had to move the new bedroom suite we had bought for Robyn's graduation gift.

This was so painful for all of us. We remembered what an ordeal we had moving her from Louisville to St. Louis—never even thinking that she would never be able to live there or work in the orphanage that had hired her. When we got to St. Louis, Ramona had all of Robyn's things packed in boxes except for Robyn's clothes, as she did not know what I wanted to do with them. After I thought for a while, I asked my husband about taking the clothes to the orphanage that had hired Robyn and donating them to the girls' there. So we packed up all Robyn's shoes and clothing, and the staff at the children's home were really happy to have it all, as they have so many needs. They were so nice and gracious to us.

Robyn had a Raggedy Ann Doll that traveled with her through high school, Anderson College (now Anderson University) and Southern Baptist Theological Seminary. She sat on Robyn's bed constantly and went through all the crazy things Robyn did. When we went to get

Robyn's things, I picked up Raggedy Ann and she was practically in strings. Her face had a tear right under the lift eye that went the length of her face. It looked like she had a tear falling down her cheek. I wanted to say to her, "I know you're crying, and so are we." I debated on putting her in Robyn's arms and at the end I said, "No, I'm going to keep her with me." I needed Raggedy Ann to remind me of Robyn and to know I've got that little part of her with me and to help me tell others about her life.

Robyn with Raggedy Ann at Seminary.

I was so thankful for Todd. At the time we lost Robyn, he was not married—still looking. During Robyn's college and seminary years, her friends came to the house very often. The girls would always question Robyn about her brother: "Who does he go out with?" "Could I get a date with him?" "How available is he?" Several of them swooned over him, but Robyn would tell them to cool it. Todd paid them no attention. We lost Robyn in 1991 and Todd got married in 1995.

After losing Robyn, Todd seemed to sense what I was going through, and he was wonderful. We talked more, and we even went shopping together—something he knew I especially liked to do—and this helped soothe the pain of losing Robyn. I will always be thankful for the special attention Todd showed at this crucial time in my life. I'm sure this was healing for him also, as he and Robyn were very close.

Robyn's friends also were so wonderful. They kept in touch with phone calls, letters, and personal notes. I don't want them ever to forget Robyn, and I tried to give her closest friends something that belonged to her. The thought occurred to me to give each of them a charm to go on a bracelet or necklace with her name on one side and Proverbs 3:5-6 on the other side. These particular verses had been some of Robyn's favorites, and were the Scripture verses I had chosen to put on her headstone.

Some of the nurses and friends Robyn made at Duke called me one day and said they were going to have a brief service for Robyn and release balloons into the air; they felt this would help release their grief for her as they symbolically released her to her heavenly Father.

When school was out in June, the dean at Southern Seminary called and said, "I just wanted you and your husband to know that Robyn was voted by her peers as the most outstanding student in the social work field." I was momentarily speechless, but when I could talk, I said, "Oh, how she would have cherished this honor. I wish she had known." The dean replied, "She knows!"

It's so hard for me, even after so many years, to look back through Robyn's things and see all her pictures. When I was going through Robyn's closet at home, I noticed a jar about half full of coins. Taped to the jar was a note: "Saving to return to Bermuda." And Robyn loved to take pictures. She took pictures everywhere she went because, here again, these were her treasured friends having such a good time at whatever they were doing.

Not long after I lost her, as I was looking through some of the things Robyn had written, I came across a long list of sixty-two names inside a plastic three-ring notebook cover. Robyn had scribbled little notes beside some of them, about a need, or a health concern, or a problem. As I contemplated exactly what this was, I read down through the names and scribbling and finally figured it out—this was Robyn's prayer list.

I was amazed. I just had to say, "Thank you, God." I'll have to admit my prayer list did not compare in length. What a continued blessing to me my daughter is.

I told God that if he healed her, we would glorify him, and if he called her to join him, we would glorify him. So many times I had heard Robyn tell her friends, "Go for it!" First Corinthians 15:58 tells me to give fully to the work of the Lord—my labor is not in vain. Now I could hear Robyn telling me, "Go for it, Mom." I needed to look for opportunities and go for it for the Lord.

God would not leave me alone about what I should do with all this. I felt so strongly that he wanted me to write about Robyn, not to magnify her but as an encouragement and influence to parents and to young people. Her friends have encouraged me to do this, and I have often been privileged to share with other parents who have lost a daughter or son. At those times I felt God was saying to me that if our story was written down, I could hand it to these hurting people as an added blessing to them and an encouragement to keep on keeping on.

I will have to say, writing this book is one of the hardest things I have ever tried to do. With God's help, I began not long after I lost Robyn, in the summers when I was out of school. I'd write a while and then have to leave it, as it was so painful to relive this again in my mind. I told myself I would finish the book when I retired from teaching. I knew William could help me later with names and details because he was such an organized detail person and had written a lot of the doctor's reports and comments down.

CHAPTER 12

"NEVER GIVE UP"

I RETIRED FROM full-time teaching in June 2001, and in December 2001, just six months later, the most painful of all my trials began. My husband became ill.

He had not retired yet from Milliken, and he had talked about so many things he wanted us to do when he retired and the places he wanted to take me. He wanted to go back to Texas to show me some of the places he had visited when he was in the army there. We really hadn't done much traveling together, since we were both working. I was always working on something for school at home, even in the summers, or I was taking a graduate course somewhere. When we did go somewhere, maybe for a weekend or, occasionally, for a week, he would ask me where I wanted to go, and I would encourage him to choose somewhere he would like to go. He would always say, "It doesn't matter where we go as long as I'm with you."

Usually, in the summer we would spend one week at the beach. William wanted us to be able to spend more time together during the year and in the summer.

William had the type of skin that got a lot of moles. His mother had this type of skin, and also his brother, and William had been under the care of a dermatologist for years. He had a small mole removed from his arm right before we moved to Spartanburg from Anderson, and the doctor said the report came back melanoma. At the time, I knew that this was a serious kind of skin cancer, but the doctor said he got all of it and did not seemed concerned because it was so small. In fact, the doctor William saw in Spartanburg said he was not sure it was melanoma.

About five years later, when he was having a routine physical, the doctor saw a small mole on William's shoulder. A dermatologist agreed that it should be removed, and I took a day off school to be with him, thinking the procedure would be two or three hours. It ended up taking all day. I would not leave the waiting room, even to eat, thinking I would hear from the doctor any minute.

It was late in the afternoon when the doctor finally called me. He said the reason the surgery had taken so long was that he had to go a lot deeper in William's shoulder than he originally thought he would have to. Then the doctor told me there was no way they could tell if the melanoma was in William's bloodstream, and I could tell he was very concerned about this possibility. He suggested we have a test to see if it was in any of the glands. He also suggested we see an oncologist. The doctor ended the conversation by saying that if the cancer was in William's bloodstream it would go to other parts of his body.

I became very concerned, but I was very positive with William. I couldn't believe that as advanced as medicine is now there was not a test that could tell us if the cancer was in his bloodstream. William had the test to see if the cancer had spread to his glands. They turned out to be clear, and we were so thankful.

All during this time, I was doing some intense praying. William's job at Milliken was very demanding and nerve-wracking. He also taught an adult couples class at church. In the meantime, I read an article in *Reader's Digest* about a melanoma vaccine. I mentioned this to several of his doctors in Spartanburg, but they had never heard of this. We were referred to a specialist at Duke. I took the article and showed it to him. He knew of a doctor who was administering the vaccine, which was in the trial stage and not FDA approved yet. We made return trips to Duke over three weeks so William could get the vaccine.

After he got through with this, William suggested we go to Hilton Head for a long weekend. Late the night before we were to leave, a friend from Anderson called me and said the principal I had worked under in Anderson, whom we all loved and respected, had just passed away. The school wanted me to speak for the teachers at her funeral. I thought so much of this principal that I almost told William I would have to do this. But after I slept on it and prayed about it, and knowing that William needed to get away, I called back and said I would write something up that another teacher could read on my behalf. I am so thankful I did this.

William had a brother in Beaufort whom he did not get to see often. He called his brother and told him to meet us at the motel and we could visit and go out to supper. The weather was nice and we enjoyed this so much.

One night on our trip, William got up in the middle of the night, which was unusual for him, and tried to open the sliding glass door that went out to the patio. I wake up easily, and I saw what he was doing. I said, "Where are you going?" He said he was going to the bathroom. I told him it was in the opposite direction.

This was not like William. William could always find his way around anywhere. It was me who had to have his help finding my way around. I was always amazed that he could find his way right back to our car in a big parking lot. It would make me mad that he was always right! Whenever we went on a trip with anyone, William was the one everyone else would follow. I knew then that something was not right, but I did not want to admit it.

When we got back, William went to see the oncologist, who told him he had a choice about his treatment: do nothing and pray the cancer was not in the bloodstream or take six months of interferon, which had side effects but was the only treatment that was offered for melanoma. The doctor went on to say that this was not a 100 percent cure, that probably only about 10 percent of patients had good results with it. But we both wanted to do all we could to stop this awful disease, so William agreed to do this.

As the treatments progressed, William got weaker and his appetite was not good. He tried so hard to keep teaching his Sunday school class, but he really did not feel like it. He eventually got so weak that he would go to work in the morning and come home after lunch and go to bed. We counted the days until he would get through the treatment.

He wanted me to have his Sunday school class to our house for a Christmas party. The week before we were to have the party, he came home early from work with a terrific headache. My heart sank. I called the doctor, and he said to take him to the emergency room and get a CAT scan. When William gave the hospital staff the information about having the moles removed and what he had been through, I could tell they were concerned. After the first scan, we were asked to stay and take a second one. We did, and the second report confirmed the first—a spot on the brain. William was given something to ease his headache and told to see the oncologist as soon as possible.

William was so depressed with this report. I was so scared but tried not to show it. I never will forget leaving the emergency room and hearing him say, "I certainly did not want to hear that news." He wanted me to go on and have the Sunday school class party on Friday and asked me to say nothing about this new situation; he would tell the class on Sunday. We had grown to know and love all the couples in that class, and they loved William.

William related well to the men in his class and they enjoyed a great camaraderie with one another. He had also done a terrific job teaching. He spent hours and hours studying the lesson. The time we could have spent together, especially on Saturdays, he was working on his lesson, getting it just the way he wanted to deliver it. Most of the time he would apply something in the lesson to a current event. He was an avid reader. Even when he watched a ball game on TV (which he loved), he would have three or four magazines or books in front of him. He had grown so much in his teaching, and everyone enjoyed the class. The class had also grown. We had several in the class who were not married but just liked to hear him teach.

We went ahead with the Christmas party, but my heart was not in it. The following Sunday, at the end of the lesson, William told the class the melanoma had returned and was in his brain. We all left in tears, including William. He was always a rock for me and so strong; I was the weak one. Many times I had gone all to pieces about something while he showed such strength. However, this was his life and his future with his family, and he couldn't understand what was happening and why it was happening to him, and neither could anyone else.

I heard Dr. David Jeremiah say that when he had cancer and was going through treatments, whenever he prayed, he would start crying. I had hardly ever seen William get emotional, but after this second ordeal and being told he had spots on his brain, every time we sat down to eat together and return thanks, he would just grab my hand, and with tears in his eyes say, "You pray."

William had been advised not to retire when he found out about the melanoma, and he was still doing his job at Milliken. After visiting the oncologist again, we were referred to Bowman Gray School of Medicine at Wake Forest University Baptist Medical Center in Winston-Salem, North Carolina for a new procedure called the gamma knife. We had never heard of this, but when we told others about it, people began sending us information about it. The wonderful thing was that it was not regular surgery but was done with a laser that pinpoints a tumor and kills it or dries it up.

We were very encouraged about this procedure, and the doctors and nurses at Bowman Gray were so encouraging and supportive. It was the best hospital we had ever had experience with. The staff were like angels. We knew by this time that we were dealing with a very serious disease that would not be easily destroyed.

We waited for several weeks for the surgery, and the day finally came. A contraption on William's head fit down over his shoulders and immobilized his head and neck. After the procedure, William was in good spirits and ate a little. He was to return for an MRI in about a month to see if the tumor had been killed.

On Sundays I would fix lunch for Todd and his family so they could be with William and he could enjoy the grandchildren. He loved playing with the grandchildren, on the floor when he felt like it. I was usually in the kitchen cooking while he entertained them with his tricks. Todd's middle son, Josh, was about three years old at the time and told me one day that "Daddy Bill" was his best buddy. Todd's daughter Audrey was five years old and the baby was one year old.

When we first went back to Bowman Gray and had the MRI, the news was inconclusive but not alarming. When we returned several months later, the MRI showed two more tumors in the brain. The oncologist in Spartanburg ordered an X-ray of the liver and colon and later called to say there was a spot on the liver. William and I were so discouraged and our spirits were low. It seemed as though every time we saw a ray of hope, another spot of melanoma turned up in William's body.

We were seeing the oncologist in Spartanburg during this time, and I was disappointed with him for many reasons. His attitude did not compare with what we had experienced at Bowman Gray and the doctors and nurses there.

William asked me to take him to Milliken to clean out his desk. I couldn't get over how neat and organized everything was and the files and files of material he kept on each mill he was responsible for. Someone would call him on the phone at home, and he would tell them which drawer and which file had what they needed. It would be there.

It was after the report on the liver that William asked me if I had ever heard the saying "Never give up." He asked me to find that for him. He also quoted the scripture about Hezekiah asking God to give him fifteen more years and God answering that prayer. He said he had prayed the same prayer, and he felt like God would do this. I found the following in his notes:

2 Kings 20—Hezekiah became ill and was at the point of death. Isaiah said, "Put your house in order; you are going to die." Hezekiah prayed. How he had walked faithfully before God and had done what was good in God's eyes with wholehearted devotion. He wept bitterly! God told Isaiah to go back and tell Hezekiah that he had heard his prayers and would heal him and that he would add fifteen years to his life and would deliver him from the king of Assyria. A sign was a shadow going backward on the steps. (Same story in Isa. 38:1–5.)

Then, he had written on Wednesday, after the review of the MRI and the doctor's report:

Romans 8:24–25, "Hope that is seen is no hope at all. Who hopes for what he already has? But if we hope for what we do not yet have, we wait for it patiently" [paraphrased].

Scripture at Sunday school:

1 John 3:21–24, "Dear friends, if our hearts do not condemn us, we have confidence before God and receive from him anything we ask, because we obey his commands and do what pleases him. And this is his command: to believe in the name of his Son, Jesus Christ, and to love one another as he has commanded us."

Philippians 4:13, "I can do everything through him who gives me strength."

Isaiah 26:3, "You will keep in perfect peace him whose mind is steadfast, because he trusts in you."

I went online and found that the phrase "Never give up" is attributed to Winston Churchill. He had attended grade school at Harrow, where he was in the lower third of his class and was considered to have no particular potential. After he graduated, however, he went on to university and eventually became famous. Near the end of his life, he was invited back to Harrow to address the student body and was introduced as one of the greatest orators of all time. The students were told to take plenty of notes. When Sir Winston addressed the boys, he said, "Young gentlemen, never give up! Never give up! Never give up! Never! Never! Never!" That was his entire address. He then sat down. I'm certain that none of those students ever forgot that advice.

And that is God's advice and word to us. If we interpret God's message to the Hebrew Christians fully, it would be, "God said, I will never, not ever, not ever leave you or forsake you" (see Hebrews 13:5). This is the greatest reason why we too must never give up.

This was a blessing to me, for I knew William's desire was to never give up.

CHAPTER 13

AN IMPORTANT LETTER

I CONTINUED TO teach until I had thirty-one years. About two months before I had retired from full-time teaching, I decided to write the district a letter and ask for a change in the sick leave policy concerning an immediate relative. If the district disagreed with me, at that point it would not matter. However, I felt the change would benefit present and future employees, most of whom were not even aware of the policy. I sent a copy to the trustees and to the superintendent of the district. The letter read:

Dear Dr. _____ :

I am writing to you concerning several pertinent matters in relation to my employment in District Six. I want to thank you and the personnel director for hiring me and allowing me to be a part of this District. Dr. _____ , you deserve congratulations and applause for leading the district in pursuing the most up-to-date curriculum and hiring competent staff and personnel to follow through with the teaching from elementary to high school. It was an honor for me to represent the district as District Teacher of the Year in 1991.

I was humbled to experience this for the second time as I had also represented District Five in Anderson in a previous year. It's so rewarding to look through my scrapbook of memories and accumulated letters from state personnel, district personnel, teachers, parents, and students from years of hard work.

Unless I feel led to change my mind, I plan to exit the classroom as an active nine months teacher. This has been a very hard decision for me, and I have given it much thought and prayer. Notice I did not say "retire" because I am not a retiring person. I feel I cannot just lay aside all the training and experience and joy of working with students, as I know I was called to teach. I will continue to substitute or work on a part-time basis and tutor. Through the years, I have seen a desperate need for the classroom teacher to have some tutorial help with that student who "falls through the cracks of testing" and has no parental support. I plan to pursue that type of program on the elementary level and can see it as fulfilling a need that has never been met. I would be happy to talk with you about this. I also plan to do some writing that I have felt I should do ever since I lost my daughter.

District Six is the fourth district I have taught in and in the third state. As previously stated, I have so many fond memories—I also have a matter of contention concerning District Six that I would like to mention. I want you to know that I can't hold a grudge and have forgiven District Six for docking my salary for two weeks when I was at Duke with my daughter for treatment on her brain tumor. Since I had, and continue to have, more than the accumulated sick leave days, I was not aware docking my salary would take place, especially since I was told I had the days. Although it will not make any difference to me now, since I am retiring, it will make a difference for the current personnel and the future teachers of District Six. So, I would simply request that you and the Board consider making a change in the personal leave and absence policy concerning terminal illness of an immediate family member. This is a matter of "lasting impression" to know how you were treated as a professional.

Could I close with some words from Paul? "I do not consider myself to have taken hold of it. But one thing I do, forgetting what is behind and straining toward what is ahead, I press on toward the goal to win the prize for which God has called me."

You never check in your "backpack" as a Christian. There is never a "bench of retirement." As long as we have strength and breath, we keep on keeping on.

Sincerely,

Martha Axmann

About two weeks before school was out, my principal walked into my room with a check in his hand. He said, "Mrs. Axmann, the superintendent wanted you to have this." When I opened the envelope, it was a check for the two weeks of docked pay when I was at Duke with Robyn! It had been ten years.

God's ways are certainly not man's ways. I did not write the letter thinking this would happen. I wanted the superintendent and my principal and the trustees of the district to know how I felt and to realize how this policy could result in negative attitudes and possibly job resignation for dedicated teachers presently employed and those who were considering joining the district.

It allowed me to leave with a better opinion about the district I had given part of my life to through years of teaching.

CHAPTER 14

EVERY REMEMBRANCE
OF YOU

WHEN WE WENT to the doctor, whether in Spartanburg or at Duke or Bowman Gray, I did all the driving. It bothered William that I had to do everything. He never had let me drive before. When we went on trips, he did all the driving. He was so good at directions and I am not. He could find anything. He just had a great sense of direction.

On one of our last visits to Bowman Gray, he was feeling so bad. He was in a wheelchair at this time because he was so weak. We left the motel to go get a sandwich for supper. I got him in the car, and we rode and rode and finally found a sandwich place, but he was not able to go in. So I went in and ordered and brought our food back to the car to take to the motel. I asked for directions before I left the restaurant, not knowing there are two streets in Durham with the same name. The clerk gave me directions to the one on the other side of town. By the time I realized I had the wrong directions, I was quite lost, and I asked William to help me find the way back. He said, "I can't. I don't know how to get back, and you've got to do it." I felt like crying. I wanted to just say, "Lord, I can't do this by myself." I kept stopping to ask for directions when traffic would allow me to. Finally, the Lord and I found the road I had originally been on, and I found my way back to the motel.

Another time, on our way back home to Spartanburg, we had to stop for gas. William had always put gas in the car and taken care of everything about the car. I never had even washed the cars. He did that. I pulled over to the tank and he started to get out of the car, but he looked at me and said, "I can't do it." To get gas did not bother me, but it broke my heart and my spirit to see William have to give up things he had always done. He was so concerned that he wasn't taking care of me.

He continued to get weaker and weaker. We were coming in the house after going to the doctor one afternoon, and he fell on the cement in the garage. He was just so weak. He caught himself with his hands; he knew he was going to fall. He immediately said, "I'm OK. I just couldn't make it another step." I could not get him up, and he still had enough pride that he did not want me to call for help. He did not want to bother anyone. None of my neighbors were home. Together we managed to get him up the steps of the garage and into the house. He kept saying, "If I just had a little more strength."

As I realized what was happening to him and as we came to grips with what all the reports were saying, William told me we were going to have to meet with a real estate lawyer and get our finances in order so I could handle them. I thought again, *I can't do this by myself.* Up to this point in our married life, I had left all of this up to him. He was so talented at finances. This was his job at Milliken; he handled the budgets for several mills, and he had always done this at home and did not want me to do it. Thank God for this time he gave him to help me plan for the future without him.

William could not talk about leaving me, and neither could I fathom life without him. We were so close. We had a beautiful marriage. When we prayed together, I would pray out loud, asking the Lord to heal him. Every night I went to sleep in his arms.

When the last MRI showed more spots in his brain and the scan showed spots on his liver, the doctors at Bowman Gray said the only thing they could do was brain radiation. We would have to go up there and stay in a motel, and I would take him back and forth each day for his radiation treatment.

This was a nightmare for me. I had already been through this once with Robyn, and the treatment had not helped. However, we were reaching for the last straw and praying for healing. Sometime right before we left to go to Bowman Gray for the whole-brain radiation, William wrote a letter to me and left it tucked under a lamp in the den near the chair where he always sat. I did not find it until after I lost him, and that was probably the way he planned it. This is what he wrote and left under the lamp:

Martha Attributes

How do you describe all the wonderful things about the wife God led you to?

You prayed for years and years for the right one, and God led you to her! The best possible thing from Furman. Your lifelong best friend, someone who always wanted to be and do the best:

Her relationship to her God.

Her vocation—the best—teach the best, bring out the best in students, strive to set an example both in preparation, training, planning, execution, and developing students.

Her children—set the example, be there for them. Participate in their activities, sound advice.

Music—all those years at Mountain Creek Baptist Church, always prepared, always willing to help others, always creative in writing, skits, improvising ways to make Christ's message more attractive, especially in musicals and inviting guests with unusual testimonies to witness to those who might not otherwise be reached.

Working with young children, especially new ones in the ministry. This goes back to the Hartsville GAs and even back to her mother's influence while growing up in Cowpens.

Husband—what can I say? How could I have even attracted such a pretty girl without God's intervention? Someone who is always attractive, someone who always strives to look her best (and does). I still need to apologize for my temper and attitude since all these steroids. I have always loved her! My parents and all my relatives have always loved her! And she treated all of them as if they were her own, especially my mom and dad. How they loved her! What a rare thing in this day and time.

If these doctors are right and the brain tumors are a recurrent problem, then my only regret is not to be able to do some of the things we wanted to do together after retirement. Just be together, travel to some places we've never been, revisit some places where we had lived before—like Connecticut! We'll just have to trust God and see what he has in store. More on this later!

Rudolph Fowler introduced me to the prettiest girl I ever met. From the first time I saw her at Furman, I wanted her. No car to date in except when Rudolph wanted to double date. What a great time!

A couple in our Sunday school class insisted on going with us to get us settled in Durham. William was in a wheelchair and getting him in and out of the car was about more than I could handle. Thank God for Christian friends. They left after we got in the motel.

I took him back and forth for treatments every day. I tried to fix something in our room for lunch and then go get something for supper. One or two times we ate in the hospital cafeteria. On one of those days, after about a week of treatment, while we were eating William said, "If these reports are right, I just can't understand what good could be gained for God to take me—we love each other so much and have so much we want to do together."

He was so down and I was too, but I tried to be positive by letting him know I was not going to give up. We were turning it over to God and asking for his healing, just like we had been doing ever since we found out that it was melanoma. The steroids, the tumors, and the treatments had made an emotional wreck out of him, taken his pride, and were gradually taking his body.

After the second week, he was so weak he could hardly hold himself up in the wheelchair, and he felt so bad. The doctor told me he would probably have to put him in the hospital. He did a blood test and said he would call me at the motel. He called later that evening and said William's blood sugar was so high that I would have to put him in the hospital the next morning. William looked at me and said, "No, I'm not going to the hospital." I could see signs every day that William was not himself. It was more evident after they started the whole-brain radiation. I tried to explain to him that we had to do what the doctor said.

That night, I prayed and prayed. I knew there were two reasons he did not want to do this. He did not want to leave me in that motel by myself, and he did not want to "give up" and go to the hospital. The next morning he felt so bad and was so weak. I packed his bag, and we went on the shuttle bus, which had a lift to accommodate William being in a wheelchair. At the hospital the doctor discussed William's blood sugar with him, and William realized he did not have a choice. He did not want to say no in front of the doctor.

Again I had to pray that God would be with me as I drove myself back and forth in a strange town and in and out of the hospital by myself. I left early in the morning and stayed as late as I could while making sure I got back to the motel before dark.

William could not shave himself. I had never shaved him, so this was a learning experience for me. My son and family came on the weekend, and I asked Todd to bring an electric razor, which worked a little better. William felt so bad that he really did not care.

After another week of radiation, the doctor said, "I'm going to send him home. We're not going to do the full six weeks."

At this time, William was taking a lot of medication, including a new drug to combat brain tumors. He also was receiving insulin for the high blood sugar. The doctor said I could do the blood sugar checks and give William shots of insulin at home.

I was overwhelmed. I had never given a shot before, and especially not to someone I loved. The nurses met with me and listed all the medications, when to give each one, and how to check William's blood sugar. I practiced giving shots with them. They told me that they had ordered the new drug to be sent to the oncologist in Spartanburg and for me to pick it up when I got home. I asked if they were sure I would be able to get it, and they assured me I would.

At this time, William could not even sit up, and I had to make a decision as to how I was going to get him home. His secretary at Milliken had kept in touch, and many of William's co-workers had sent cards and flowers to the motel where we were staying. The secretary had told me that Milliken would do anything that would be helpful to us. She asked me if I needed the Milliken plane to get William home, and I said I would talk to William about it. I tried to talk with him, and he said, "No, don't ask for the plane." But Todd and I decided we did not have a choice. We asked for the plane to come and get us.

I was so upset about all this. Trying to please William and trying to understand exactly what I was to do about all the medication and giving it properly—I was in tears at this point. I tried to dress William for the trip. He would look at me so strangely at times—he just wasn't himself. I had to get an ambulance to take him to the airport, and I told the driver not to lose me, that I would be right behind him in my car, and if he lost me I would never find my way. I had no idea where the airport was in Durham.

Todd flew to Durham and drove my car back to Spartanburg, and I went with William on the plane. The men on the plane were so gentle with William and placed him in the plane in a reclining chair, and I sat right beside him in a regular seat. I had never flown before, and I was so thankful that my first flight was with William. The beauty of the sky amazed me.

While we were in North Carolina, our Sunday school class had come and built a ramp out our back door for William to use with the wheelchair. I couldn't believe it. My son and daughter-in-law had a carpenter put up special rails in the bathroom and up the stairs and had a hospital bed brought in. The Sunday school class also had arranged for an ambulance to meet us at the airport and bring us home. The two firemen with the ambulance looked at me as they were leaving and said, "If you ever need us, just call."

I went immediately and got all William's prescriptions filled. I was in for another shock when I called the oncologist's office about the drug I had been told would be in Spartanburg when I got there. I was informed that the doctor in Spartanburg was not going to give the drug to William; there was no need. I was furious. With all I had been through at this point, I did not need another problem. I called the doctor at Bowman Gray and finally got him and told him what had occurred, and I asked him if he would talk with the doctor in Spartanburg. He did and I got the drug.

In the meantime, the doctor in Spartanburg asked if he could come to our home and talk with William. Of course, I told him he could. But instead of trying to encourage William at this crucial time, he more or less told him to give up, that there was nothing else doctors could do, and that he did not see any need for William to take the medication. As I have said, William was not himself at this time, and I'm sure he had already come to the realization during the radiation treatments that he wasn't getting any better. He was a very smart person. However, no one wants to hear what this doctor was saying, and none of us want to give up. It would have been so much more fulfilling, although we knew the potential outcome, to focus our minds on a positive note.

After William heard the doctor, he said, "Oh, I did not realize… oh, I didn't know—would everyone get around me and let's pray." He thanked God for life, for the love of his family, and the many blessings he had enjoyed. But William *did* know. He had written a note about it previously.

William continued to be restless. He would slip down in the bed, and I would pull and pull, trying to get him back up. I would try to roll him to one side and then the other to change the bed. I was constantly trying to keep the bed clean. His blood sugar was so high, and he did not want me to give him his shots, and I could not get him to eat anything. He just wasn't himself. At night, I would hear him flopping around, and I would jump up and try to get him comfortable in the bed as best I could.

One night, he got his leg out through the bar of the bed, and I tried and tried to get it back. He could not help me; he just looked at me so strangely. I knew at this point I was going to have to have help. I talked with my son, and we took him to the cancer center at the hospital.

He was there only two days and nights. The second day, while I sat by his bed, his breathing was labored. I reached for a pad and pencil and started to plan his service. I thought through the whole service, what I wanted, whom I wanted, and the music.

When I finished it, I was so upset and exhausted that I felt I had to get outside and talk to God. I feel closer to God when I am outside. I walked out by the pond at the hospital where it is so quiet. There was an arbor and pretty flowers there. I lifted my face to the clouds and prayed, "Lord, you know my heart. I've prayed for you to heal him, but if that's not your will, please don't let him continue to suffer." My daughter-in-law came out to me, and we walked back in the hospital together. My son came to me in the hall and said, "Mom, he's gone." We all embraced, and I walked into the room and kissed William. This was May 25, 2002.

Sometimes God's answers are so painful, and yet we know he is with us. God's presence and power enable us to endure what comes.

My pastor met me at my home. He said, "Martha, let's go in and plan Bill's service." I said, "It's already planned." God had helped me plan it so it could be a blessing to others and a tribute to William.

William had worked for Milliken for forty-two years and had been a counselor for many of his fellow workers there. He would often come home and tell me about someone who asked to meet him in the conference room and talk after work. He was so loved and respected at his job. I wanted his life to speak to some whom I knew were hurting and were not Christians.

I asked Dr. Lee Royce, president of Anderson College at the time, to speak. William had served as trustee and chairman of the board at Anderson. I asked a member of his couples Sunday school class to speak, and also a co-worker from Milliken and a neighbor William had talked with many times in the garden at our home. William loved to work in that garden and relieve his frustrations from work. He loved the Gaither Men's Quartet, so I asked a men's quartet from our church to sing. I thank God for helping me "get it together" at the most difficult time in my life.

A few days after the funeral, I walked by the chair where he always liked to sit, and found and read the letter that I shared earlier in this chapter. To this day, I am so thankful William had the intuition to do that. I keep the letter in a special place because this is more like the man I fell in love with. If he had waited any longer, he would not have been able to write anything. He was never the same after radiation began.

What a man, what a husband, what a provider and helpmate he was to me. I thank God still for allowing me to be William's wife and for my children and grandchildren to have such a father as this. On his headstone, I had inscribed Philippians 1:3, "I thank my God upon every remembrance of you." NKJV

Can I understand it? No. But I can say as I pray for strength each day that God is with me, and my prayer is that I would do with my life now what God would have me to do.

This was the Christmas Card I designed to send to friends after I lost William.

Philippians 1:3
I thank my God everytime
I remember you!

God is
my refuge
and strength

Thank you for your prayers of
support and love!

May we show the joy of <u>Christmas</u> <u>love</u>
throughout every season of our lives.

Merry Christmas to you
in 2002
The Axmann's

Picture of my husband and myself

CHAPTER 15

ON MY OWN

I FEEL I need to say something to widows at this point. I am different now. I have to do things I had never done by myself. Let me impress upon you the importance of trying to prepare yourself to be independent in case something does happen to your mate. I have to make decisions that I never thought I would have to make by myself. At first, I could not stand to stay by myself, but I knew I had to do it. The bills started coming in constantly. These were not just one-line bills; they were pages and pages, and it was so confusing.

Milliken changed insurance companies while William was at Bowman Gray, and that made it more confusing. I am so thankful to this day for William's secretary at Milliken, who said to me, "Martha, we will file all the insurance papers—just send them to me." So I was constantly taking these huge stacks of medication bills and doctor bills and hospital bills and laboratory bills to her, and they kept coming for months. We had bills from two ambulance companies; from Duke, Bowman Gray, and Spartanburg Regional, and bills from the doctors William had seen at each of those places. Spartanburg Regional Hospital turned my account over to a collection agency because I was advised not to pay any of the bills until everything was filed and each insurance company had paid.

Then I was faced with the finances of the home and everyday life. I had never balanced the checkbook or paid the bills at home because my husband took care of all that. My son and daughter-in-law helped me the first month. I did not know at this time what William had paid monthly and what was on automatic draft. Then a friend showed me how to do some of this on the computer. After I got used to it, this was a blessing.

I lost sleep over taxes, which William had always done for us. The last couple of years he had done most of the paperwork and then taken it to a CPA in town, a man from our church. I called him up and told him I had to have help. So he told me what to do, and he kept me out of jail! He has been a constant help to me.

Then there was taking care of the yard and cars. William always knew what the cars needed and when they needed it. He even kept them in gas and washed them. With all the housework, and trying to learn finances, I really did not have time to wash the car and keep the yard like I knew it should be tended to. I found a good place to wash the car, and I asked the dealer to show me how I could know what needed to be checked and when. They have done that.

I still struggle with repairs for the house and work in the yard. I have allergies and the yard work makes it worse. But I try to do some, and I get help with the rest.

It seems when I come up against an obstacle or have an attitude of giving up, God has put someone in my path to help me. Sometimes I want God to just audibly tell me what he wants me to do and then I could be certain I'm in his will. But it's amazing at times how I have felt his direction in where I was, or what someone said to me, or through prayer, Bible study, and meditation.

After I lost William, and as I thought about his term as trustee at Anderson College and how useful he had been there, it just came to me that I should finish out his term. I couldn't believe I did it, but one day I called the chairman of the board and volunteered to finish William's term. The board welcomed me with open arms. When I went for the first meeting, I found myself in a beautiful room, sitting at a huge table with mostly men, many of whom were pastors, and I thought, *what am I doing here?* That day an Anderson College student came in right at the beginning of the meeting to give a devotional. He said, "My scripture today is from Proverbs 3:5–6."

I couldn't believe it. Those verses had become my favorite and were the ones I had put on Robyn's headstone. He went on and talked about trust. He pointed out that whatever you were going through, to look for opportunities. We don't have to solve everything; we can rely on the Lord. He gave the example of a parachute: the only way to find out if it works is to leap and see if the parachute opens. He reminded us to "lean not unto thine own understanding," but to call on God, and "in all thy ways acknowledge him." KJV He's already working in the future. We must depend on God.

The speaker also used an example of a little boy who was in a candy store with his nose pressed up to the candy counter. The owner said, "You can get some; reach in."

The little boy said, "No, you get it for me with your hand." The owner wanted to know why, and the little boy said, "If I use my hand, it would only be a small amount, but if you use your hand, it will be more." Use God's hand—trust him.

Well, I knew God was telling me I was in the right place.

When summer came and I wanted to go to the beach as we had always done, I had negative thoughts: *I guess I won't even be able to go on vacation again because I won't go by myself.* However, my son and his family have included me in their vacations, and I have traveled some with a lady friend from my church. It's not the same, because I miss my husband so much, but at least I'm not sitting home by myself all the time.

The loneliness still creeps in and is constant. I lost Robyn in 1991 and William in 2002. I just try to stay busy with tutoring, church work, and doing for others. Some days, when I feel blue or something reminds me of William or Robyn, I try to get out and do something for someone else. It helps me feel better. I still will not go out to eat by myself or go some places I would like to go because I will not go by myself.

I feel like a broken pot of clay that God needs to put back together. The following poem expresses my thoughts.

> I feel just like a broken pot
> worthless, cracked and peeled
> then SOMEHOW I heard a voice that said—
> "Let's place you on my wheel."
>
> He said "My life has paid the price."
> He placed me on His wheel—
> And with the potter's, nail-pierced hands
> he began to shape and heal.
>
> I feel my life renewed again!
> And I was made to see
> That when life's trials brake me down—
> The potter remolds me.
>
> Praise God, he reveals His sovereignty
> In a life that's cracked and peeled—
> thank God for the Master Potter
> When my life to Him I yield!

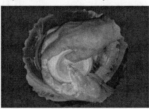

Jeremiah 18: 2-4, "Go down to the potter's house and there I will give you my message." So I went down to the potter's house, and I saw him working at the wheel. But the pot he was shaping from the clay was marred in his hands: so the potter formed it into another pot, shaping it as seemed best to him.

Isaiah 64: 8, Yet O Lord, you are our Father. We are the clay, you are the potter; we are the work of your hand.

CHAPTER 16

FOR PARENTS AND
YOUNG PEOPLE

SOMETIMES AS PARENTS we feel as though our efforts are in vain, but we are creating a path for our young people to follow. We are setting the example for them. They are watching everything we do.

Every child deserves a foundation of Christian principles laid down and secured by Christian parents. You are their pattern. Stay as close to your children as you possibly can. There are many things we can do to teach our children these Christian principles, but we need to keep the lines of communication open. We can be their friend, but at the same time we must also be their leader. As the leader, we command respect and love. Let your children know their limitations. Let them know what you require of them. Show an interest in them and what they like. Be there for them. Build a relationship with your kids. Play with them—ball, ping-pong, board games. It's surprising the values you can teach and advice you can give while playing a game, and you are creating a bond between yourself and your child. As you talk about the rules of the game, apply them to the rules you expect as a parent. Without realizing it, you are building a relationship, and your children will want to please you.

Encourage them when they are down or overloaded. Life is so short. Take advantage of the time they are under your care and guidance. Help them choose the right friends and conduct. Try to be a part of their activities when possible. Don't protect them from consequences; let them learn from their mistakes. Let them know what you expect and why.

Talk with their friends. It's surprising what you will find out by getting to know their friends. Be patient with their current trends and fashions, but still let them know your limitations. Encourage them to participate in youth and mission opportunities in your church or other churches.

There are so many good books on parenting. Read and stay in tune with them. Through the years, I have been a constant student of Dr. James Dobson through his radio program and books. His advice is so valuable, true, and tested.

I am not a perfect parent, but I thank God for the privilege of having had the experience. William and I decided when we started our family that I would not teach until our children were old enough to attend school. I stayed at home with them until Robyn was in second grade. I took her to a church kindergarten where I taught. As William and I looked back over her life and how she gave of herself to others in Christ's work in such a short time, we had so much to be thankful for. We were privileged to be the parents of two children and watch them grow and respond to God's leading and direction.

We will never understand why God allowed this to happen. Knowing Robyn's determination and zest for life, her influence on others and the beauty with which she displayed it, it made little sense. God has given us his mercy and peace in knowing he had to have her. I felt the holiness of God as she breathed her last breath; we were on holy ground. I had a peace at that moment that this was God's business and not to disturb.

There is one message I would like to leave with young people. *Walk with God every step of the way.* No matter if you're ten or twenty-five; your age doesn't matter. Don't think that because you are young your life is all in front of you and you have many years to live. You could be told today you have an illness that will snuff out your life. You could be in an accident and not live to tell about it. I've seen it happen again and again.

Robyn loved life and lived it to the fullest. She had so many aspirations and goals, so much she looked forward to being a part of. I know she would not want me to go around in doom and gloom. She does not want me to be sad. Each day is a blessing, young people. Get up and give it to God and live it to the fullest! Have fun in the right way—in God's way. Robyn is probably looking down at me saying, "Poopsie, you write down all those good things about me in a book and bring it with you when you come to heaven."

Again, to show you Robyn's personality, here is a note Robyn wrote to me and left on the kitchen counter when I was at school as she left with her dad for the first week of radiation treatments:

> Dear Mom,
> Don't have any wild parties tonight. We will find out about it! Vic will tell us. You ought to take a long bubble bath and just relax! I have some string music in my tape case—so soothing you know!
> Don't relax too much. You need to take all my calls from my boyfriends. Ha! You can schedule them in next week.
> Don't walk after dark and keep the door locked when you come in!
> I love you,
> Robyn

She knew I like to take a walk at night, and Vic was our neighbor.

My message is not to scare anyone, but we need to realize that age makes no difference in how many days we have here on this earth. Give your life—all of it—to God today and know that you are in his will, and he will take care of the rest. "In all your ways acknowledge Him and He shall direct your paths." (Proverbs 3:5–6) NKJV I was amazed at how many graduating seniors at my church chose these verses as a life verse more than any others.

Just recently, a young person at my church, a senior at North Greenville College, was killed instantly in a car accident on Highway 11. Something very similar happened to another student at Anderson. She was going to a ball game with two other friends. The car had a flat tire, and she was thrown from the car and killed. Examples like this show us that the future is uncertain.

Young people, give God thanks for each day and ask his direction about how you should use it. At the end of each day, we should be able to say, "I gave it my best today, for you God! Here's my offering."

Whether you realize it or not, someone is watching you, and you are influencing him or her either in a good or bad way.

You remember the little boy, Jonathan, I wrote you about in previous chapters? Robyn was his nanny for about three and a half years. Jonathan and his family have kept up with Todd and me. For a long time after Robyn's death, I sent him a gift at Christmas and remembered his birthday because I felt this was something Robyn would want me to do. They had a special relationship. He did turn out to be a very exceptional student in school, skipping several grades as Robyn had predicted. When he finished high school, he sent me an invitation to his graduation. I went through Robyn's things and took out pictures of him and Robyn when he was a baby. She had taken albums of pictures. I tried to include parties and different events they had celebrated together at Jonathan's home. I also typed out several things Robyn had written in her journal that I knew he would enjoy. I made a collage with all of this and had it framed as his graduation present. I found a verse on a card Robyn had saved that sounded like she was thinking of Jonathan, and I placed it under his graduation announcement, with a picture of him today:

You have a strong and beautiful spirit within you—
A spirit that is capable of taking you
As far and as high as you want to go.

I have seen so many of your strengths.
I appreciate your wisdom, courage, wit, and loving nature.
I know there are great things out there for you,
And it's within your power to make them happen.

This is the thank-you note Jonathan sent me after receiving the collage:

Dear Mrs. Axmann:

I really don't know how I can begin to thank you for your marvelous collage of the photographs of Robyn and me, the quotes from Robyn's journal, and the note you wrote me—opening the gift was such an emotional experience for my mother and me that I can't imagine how much more emotional compiling it must have been for you.

It was wonderful and overwhelming to see all those pictures of Robyn and me together in one place, and it was especially nice that you included the baby picture of Robyn and Todd, the photos of her with her friends, and the quotes from her journal, none of which I had ever seen before, and all of which helped to supplement my own memories. I promise you that I will love and cherish your gift forever. I hope you understand how much I appreciate it, as I am more grateful than words can really express.

I was greatly saddened to hear of Mr. Axmann's passing and I send you my sincere condolences. I hope that you are doing all right and feeling well. Thank you again for your gift, and I love you.

Love, Jonathan

Mr. & Mrs. Axmann,

My name is Becki Anderson I belong at Highland Park First Baptist Church, Robyn was my youth minister. I just wanted to tell you what a fantastic daughter you had! I don't know if Robyn knew what an influence she has had over me. When I first heard Robyn was sick I didn't know what to think. I asked "why Robyn, Lord," I knew that Robyn was a wonderful person and could do a lot in this world to make it better, but "I let go and let God," so to speak and I prayed for her and now the Lord has taken her to her reward in heaven. I know Robyn's Mansion is just beautiful in heaven.

In Sunday School Robyn told us when she was in High School there was a girl that she really admired and wanted to be like well Robyn's the person I want to be like, and I hope someday I can be an influence to a young person, like she has been to me! I know that losing her has been hard on all of you, but when the pain gets really bad, just look to God and he'll help you weather the storm (I guess you already know this!)

CHAPTER 17

OUR RESPONSIBILITY

WE EACH HAVE a responsibility for how we use the time, talents, and gifts God has given us. I felt a responsibility to God to tell this story even though it brought my depression back. However, as I have gone through this trial, I know God has been with me all the way, and I am a stronger Christian in many ways. I still have a lot of learning to do and a lot of room for growing in my Christian life. Every day I ask for God's direction and guidance and that he would strengthen my faith.

Some of you reading this can sympathize because you have suffered a similar loss and felt the pain. Some will ask, "Why, Lord? How could one so young accomplish so much and be such an influence, train to the best of her ability, and then her life is snuffed out?" Some young person reading this who is searching—maybe even dropped out of school, maybe with some skeleton in their closet that they hope stays hidden—might be inspired by Robyn's story. You may even say you want to turn your life around and be a Robyn. Some of you may have a major personal problem that you feel has you by the nape of the neck and will be the ruination of you and your loved ones; you have given up on life. Yet you see the determination and joy Robyn had in her everyday walk in life with God. You can determine to turn from that problem and say, "I want to experience that day-to-day joy Robyn had in Christ. I'm going to turn this problem over to God."

Some of you may read the book and shut it and walk back into the love and warmth of your family circle and say, "This won't happen to me and mine." Don't think you are immune to death knocking on your door and taking you or someone in your family. Somehow, in my limited vision of God, I felt that if I gave my life to him and lived for him as best as I knew how, my family and I would have the opportunity to live our "four and twenty" years together serving him. I had endured the loss of my mother and father, and as bad as that was, I knew they had lived some eighty years and made their contribution. But when my child and my husband were taken, I wrestled with God in a way I never had before.

I heard a professional football player say that the players on his team were judged by the YAC—yards after contact. When you've been contacted by the devil after sickness, after ridicule, after loss, how do you act as a Christian? Do you grow? Are you stronger? You should be; we fight harder, and it makes us stronger Christians. The speaker gave an example of a boxer whose opponent was much stronger and bigger than he was, but he was determined to fight him. Each round, the "little man" was getting beat up, and the referee kept asking him, "Don't you want to call the fight?"

"No," he would say, "just one more round." The fight went twenty-five rounds, and in the last round the little man knocked the other boxer out.

The devil is against us and we need to say, "Just one more round."

I know God is going to use this message I am trying to convey for his glory, and I know it will change some lives. I praise God for allowing me to go "just one more round" for his glory! I have prayed for God to give me the wisdom to do what he would have me to do. Now I pray you will receive from this book the inspiration you need, and do with it what God would have you do. That's your responsibility. I pray that you would experience that joy in Christ. I am so thankful for that joy in the Lord that Robyn and my husband exemplified in their lives.

"[Trials] have come so that [our] faith may be proved genuine" (1 Peter 1:7). As a song by Andraé Crouch says, "Through it all, through it all, I've learned to trust in Jesus, I've learned to trust in God."

Through It All

I've had many tears and sorrows,
I've had questions for tomorrow;
There've been times I didn't know right from wrong.
But in every situation God gave blessed consolation
that my trials come to only make me strong.

I thank God for the mountains
And I thank Him for the valleys,
I thank Him for the storms
He brought me through,
For if I'd never had a problem I wouldn't know
that He could solve them,
I'd never know what faith in God could do.

Chorus:
Through It All, Through It all,
Oh I've learned to trust in Jesus,
I've learned to trust in God—
Through It all, Through It all
I've learned to depend upon His word.

Letters of Comfort
and Inspiration

ROBYN KEPT A daily journal up until she went to Florida with her grandparents. She came back so weak and sick that she was no longer able to record her thoughts. The last day she wrote in her journal was on February 12, 1991, and she died on March 11, 1991. Her last entry was about how hard it was to find something part-time in social work! She was still hopeful and trying to pursue what she had her heart set on doing until she could get to the job she had been hired to do.

Robyn believed in doing her work, but she also believed in sharing good times with friends as often as she could. It seemed that her leadership and organizational characteristics surfaced in every situation. It was difficult for her to say no to anoyone who asked her to do something.

After losing her, I was gradually made more aware and humbled by the letters I received from people. Some of these people I had never personally met, but I had heard Robyn speak about them. Some of the notes were sent to Robyn to encourage her and express to her how she influenced their lives. They are an inspiration to me. Perhaps they will also be an inspiration to you.

Ecclesiastes 4: 9-10 "Two are better than one, because they have a good return for their work: If one falls down, his friend can help him up. But pity the man who falls and has no one to help him up!"

Robyn,
I just recieved your letter the day after your surgery. It touched me deeply. Robyn, your faith and endless strength are incredible and the rest of your friends are also. It causes me to reflect back on your response to the shocking news of the lump on your breast. I firmly believed that this experience has helped you deal with your present crisis. It has strengthened your response to your tumor. You have strengthened me as well. Numerous times I have leaned upon you in times of depression. One time in a particular, I remember when you

embraced me at my bedside
when I was absolutely
hopeless. You comforted,
supported, and guided me.
I am grateful that
I can now be there
for you at any time!
If I can be of any
help to your parents
and Todd, let me know.
Robyn, you are so blessed
in that so many people
love you and are
constantly praying for
you. And I know you
realize that, but I
am blessed in that I
am privileged to be
one of them.

I have Keep Holding On ♫♪
I wrote this
during my
philosophy class.

Robyn
Love you bunches!
Glo-

Roommate at P.C. that
married the governor's son.

you are
one of a kind.

Thank you so much for
being a part of my special
day, Robyn! You are one of a
kind just as the card says.
Words can never express to you
how much I love you and
cherish our friendship. The Lord
truly blessed us by letting our
paths cross, didn't He? You are
wonderful — a forever friend!

July 1, 1989

I love you,
Brooke

8/31/90

Dear Robyn,

Hope this weekend provides you with lots of laughs and that your wonderful sense of humor will give you, in part, strength for whatever lies ahead of you. You are constantly in my thoughts and prayers. I'm really looking forward to the time when all this stuff is behind you and we'll get to spend more time together. I really miss you! You've become a special friend in a short amount of time.

I'm sorry that all this has come into your life. It really stinks, but I know that you can find comfort in your relationship to Christ as he is with you all the way. He promises in Hebrews 13:5 that he'll never leave us or abandon us. Hang on to that!

Hope to see you real soon.

I love you!

Angela

My help comes from the Lord,
who made heaven and earth.

Psalm 121:2

149

Robyn,
Thinking of you today
and praying that God
will keep you in his
care.
We love you and think
of you often.
Everyone at Highland Park
wishes you a speedy
recovery!

P.S. We had "special" prayer
for you Sunday in our
S.S. class! (Because
you're special!)

Dear Martha

I thought of you and Robin when I heard this week of the soldier who wrote a letter to his mother to be opened if he didn't come back from the Gulf. When the mother opened and read the letter it said, "Now, mom, I know something you don't know: I know what heaven is like."

My prayers, Martha, are for you and yours.

May God bless
and Comfort

Sarah Laudis Martin
West

P.S. Mama sends her sympathy she's doing fine in the nursing home near me.

March 16, 1991

YOU CAN BE ASSURED
OF MY CONSTANT PRAYERS
AND IF NEEDED,
I AM HERE.

Love,
Bud & Bruce Conrad

PHILIPPIANS 20:25

Dear Robyn,

We have prayed for you and your family
constantly all through
the days we are learning
of the physical problems
that have been discovered.
We have dared to pray
that you will soon be
in Greenacres, but that
most of all you will
be so aware of God's
loving care and protection
and strength.

Our state convention
staff (there are 9 of us
including secretarial staff)
has adopted you as our

152

10/16/90

Dear Robyn —

I am sorry it has taken me so long to get this note to you. But please know you have been on my heart and in my prayers. I know you are a fighter and will beat this thing with the Lord's help.

I do want you to know how thankful I am to know you. You were a ray of sun-light for me from my first day back here at seminary. You are a joy and have a way of touching every life you come in contact with.

I am trying to keep up with how you are doing through people who are able to keep in touch. I know it is impossible for you to respond to all those who are in touch with you. So don't think I expect you to. Just know that I love you and I am praying for you. Take care of yourself and listen to your doctor. Rest in knowing that many are praying for you.

His love — mine

Lacky

Phil. 1:3

Thank you for being such a special
friend. I couldn't have Asked for a better person
to be my roommate. I know the Lord Knew what
what he was doing when he put us together. Robyn
I don't know what I would have done
At AC. w/o you. Thanks for always being there.

I Love you,
Stacey
(syty)
Ms. Fairmont

Robyn, (20) look at the lips on
this baby from kissing
who.

Happy Birthday
you, sex symbol, passion pig,
sexdog, not to mention Love goddess.
your a WOMAN NOW! Ha Ha !!!
now you dont have to look up to me HA Ha Ha
anymore because I'm so much older
& more mature, your over the hill too!
XOXO   old maids

does this make you feel
better?.

sexy !....

AM GREETINGS CORP.
VG. II.   U.S.A.   MCMLXXXII, MCMLXXXIII

DEPARTMENT OF RELIGION, GREEK,
AND PHILOSOPHY

Professor from P.C.

Presbyterian College

CLINTON, SOUTH CAROLINA 29325 • (803) 833-2820

September 25, 1990

Dear Robyn,

Word has gotten to us that you are home and dealing with a severe neurological illness. I wanted to write to let you know of our concern and that you have prayer partners at the Trancau household. This must be very hard to deal with after all those years in school and when you're into your first full-time professional job! (We're just sorry that Thornwell couldn't sell itself to you!) I hope and know that you are getting lots of support from home and church. Be assured that your PC network is also supporting you.

We love you,

Jack (KPP)

Robyn,

I just want you to know that
you are very special to me. I hope
you realize I am committed to praying
for you along with the rest of your
seminary family.

Robyn, it amazes me how I walk
around campus <u>continually</u> hearing
people talk and ask eachother about your
progress. Robyn, we really care for you
and we love you very much. Please
know that we are with you and
supporting you through this time.

In Him,

Benji

Robyn:
Thanks for all the
hard work you do and
for the influence you
have had on Shannon.
We appreciate everything
you do!
May God continue to
richly bless you!

Young Person
at Spring Mountain

Dearest Robyn,

I'm sitting here writing you this letter as thoughts race through my mind. It's so hard to be a part while you're still hanging on. Its hard to turn off the special feelings I have for you my friend, not turn them off in a bad way, I could never do that but so I can go for happy — Do you understand? Its hard expressing your feelings. There seems to be so many that I don't know where to begin. I'm not doing a very good job, but in order for me to go to sleep I need to write my feelings down. I feel empty — I know it is a temporary feelings an that I will see you soon but it feels like good by. I was never real good at saying good by, even for a short while.

You'll never know the joy you have brought into my life. You have been so giving of yourself. Your smile and your laughter brighten the world around me. your hugs encourage me and make me feel like I'm somebody. You have a

special gift of making people feel
loved - Thank you. Thank you
for sharing with me all the
special qualities you have. You...
You speak, feel and give from
the heart. God placed you in my
life for a precious reason, one in
which sometimes I feel as though
I'm not very deserving of. I love
you Robyn Axmann for you are
my precious constant friend.
Depending on you is one of the
easiest but most difficult things
for me. It scares me sometimes.
Insecurity is my second nature.
I pray our friendship will only
grow to be more special through
time. I feel closer to you than
anyone in my life right now and
leaving knowing that is hard.
I could go on forever about
how much you mean to me
and how real friendship is
through knowing you. You always
give without a purpose or motive
and thats a gift in itself.
Sharing myself with you has only
been easy because of the kind
of person you are. I will miss
you greatly and my heart will

loss. Without you I have many
friends and I miss them but
spending so much time with you
is why it is so hard to leave.
When you're use to someone, especially
someone as precious as you, the
impact is greater. Well I
guess I'll close - Continuing
this would be easy but my

heart speaks louder than my words
so I'll leave it at that. The heart
finds so much beauty within that
the by will never see. You'll
be a friend for always because
you've captured my heart and
that has made all the difference
I love you Straight from
my heart.

Alisha

These are random thoughts that
just came out on paper so if
it babbles on and doesn't quite
fit into a precise neat letter
just remember it all came
from within - Emotions can be
confusing at times.

Love is
great when
shared with a friend
like you

April 1, 1991

The Axmann Family
308 Woodgrove Trace
Spartanburg, SC   29301

Dear Mr. and Mrs. Axmann, and Todd:

I was one of Robyn's classmates in the Social Work program
at Southern Seminary-- graduating in May of 1990. It was
a demanding degree, as I am sure Robyn shared, and we were
all very proud to have "made it"!

This picture of our "F.I.G." (Families, Individuals, &
Groups) class was taken on the last day that we met. . .
I think our smiles say it all!

As we all continue to process her loss, it is SO important
to remember the VICTORIES as well! I wanted to be sure
that you had a copy of this picture because it _does_
commemorate ONE of Robyn's MANY victories. She was _quite_
a lady!!!

I will continue to keep _each_ of you in my prayers-- for
strength, hope, and that peace "which passes all
understanding." Please know that you are not alone in
your suffering.

Most Sincerely,

Lou Cain

Lou Cain

The FIG Class Picture at Seminary

Dear Mr. + Mrs. Axmann,
We want you to know how much we admired Robyn. She and our son, Phillip, were classmates at P.C., and she was in our home several times with the FCA.
After graduation, we saw her in Greenwood at Ruth and Steve Riley's wedding. Then we saw her at Southern Seminary when we went to visit our other son, Russ. She was admired and loved by all who knew her. May God strengthen you during your loneliness.

"The Lord is nigh unto them that are of a broken heart."
— Psalm 34:18

Love,
Helen Dean
3-21-91

Prayer is a gift that is given . . .
when words are too deep
to be spoken.

Praying with you
during this difficult time.

With love and prayers,
Rev. + Mrs. Russell Dean
First Baptist Church - Clinton

March 24, 1991

Dear William and Martha,

You have been in my thoughts and prayers daily. From my close association with Margueriete and Sterling over the past five years I am aware of some of the emotional frustrations you are experiencing. I remember the disbelief, the loneliness, the despair, the anger, the doubts, and the ever present why?

Robin had accomplished more in her twenty five years than most people accomplish in a life time. She had prepared herself deligently to serve her Lord and mankind in a most needed field. I join you in questioning why she was not given an opportunity to use her abilities. I think it's human for us to question. I certainly don't have any answers. I only know that I love you

(over)

165

and I care about your pain. The loss of a child has to be the most difficult loss you can experience because you lose a part of yourself and you lose your future. What I'm experiencing with Melissa right now can only be a taste of what you're experiencing. May God be with you as you love each other through the loss.

Martha, Margueriete, Linda, and I hope to see you sometime during the week of April 1st. I'll be in touch.

With much love,
Shirley

Jesus loves you —
        You're not alone
With such a friend
        To call your own...
And whatever waits
        Ahead for you,
May "His promise"
        See you through.

Love,
    Bill, Judy, Chad & Sandra

work and he must have known,
she had "finished" that work!
    She was very special and
will always be remembered with
love!
            friends in Christ,
                Judy Evans

167

Dear Mr. & Mrs. Axmann,   4-2-91
    I've written this letter to you many times
in my head - there's so much I want to say to
you. I think the main thing I want to say,
though, is that I feel for you so much. I know
how sad I feel at losing a wonderful friend.
I can't even imagine the sorrow you feel at
losing a daughter - especially someone like Robyn.
Robyn was an extra-special person! I just feel
the need to share with you some things about
Robyn that I experienced in having her for a
friend. I hope that in some small way these
words will be a comfort to you, although I
know that right now these words may only
remind you more of your loss. I have been
reading a book by a man whose son died.
He speaks of the letters from friends arriving,
each expressing appreciation for his son. He
states:

> They all made me weep again: each
> word of praise a stab of loss. How
> can I be thankful, in his gone-ness,
> for what he was? I find I am. But
> the pain of the "no more" outweighs
> the gratitude of the "once was."

He goes on to say, however, that remembering is
so important:

> It means not forgetting him. It
> means speaking of him. It means
> remembering him. Remembering: one

168

one of the profoundest features
of the Christian and Jewish way
of being-in-the-world and being-
in-history is remembering. "Remember,"
"do not forget," "do this as a
remembrance." We are to hold the
past in remembrance and not let
it slide away. For in history we
find God.

In remembering Robyn, I find God because
Robyn lived a life of faith in him, and it
reminds me that I, too, should live my
life with that kind of faith. So, then, allow
me to share with you some things I remember
about Robyn.

First of all, Robyn was one of the most
"alive" persons I have ever known. If someone
asked me to name someone who really knew how
to enjoy life, my response would be Robyn. Although we knew each other all three years at
Southern, it was not until the summer of '89
that we really became close friends. I'll always
remember sitting in my dorm room and hearing
Robyn calling my name down the hall long before
she got to my room saying, "Ramona, it's time
to stop studying and go shopping"(or to a
movie, or out to eat, or just to talk). I
tended to get a little too intense and stressed
out about studies. Robyn really taught me
how to loosen up and enjoy life more. I will

169

always be grateful to her for that.

Robyn also knew, though, when it was time to be serious. She grappled with so much (as you well know) while she was at seminary. She really agonized over what to do at her church when she found out that one of the members was a 'homosexual. She wanted to be a loving Christian to this person, but she also felt a deep obligation to do the right thing. She felt that it was her responsibility as youth minister to protect those kids and make sure there were positive role models for them. She discussed the situation many times with me and other friends. She prayed about it a lot. I told her at the time that I really respected her for her serious thought, consideration and prayer about this matter.

Robyn also worked so hard as a social worker at the children's home in Louisville. She always went the extra mile in meeting with families and kids - she put in a lot more than the 20 hrs. per week required for field placement!

Robyn talked about y'all a lot. She was always excited when she got a letter or a phone call from you. She worried about you working too hard. She was always talking about how grateful she was for all you did to help her out while she was in school. I remember one time we were talking about the troubled kids we work with, and Robyn said, "Ramona, we are so blessed to have such caring and loving families."

Mrs. Axmann, Robyn used to tell me how close you and she were. She said that in church you would both get tickled about the same things and that all she had to do was look at you and you would both start laughing! She respected your opinion a lot on the guys she dated. We might be discussing one of them, and she would say, "Well, I talked to Mom and she thinks..."

I've never seen Robyn as excited as when y'all and her grandparents came to visit her at Southern last year. She wanted all of us to be there to meet you and visit with you. She was so proud of you! She felt the same when Todd came to visit.

She struggled so hard with the decision to come to St. Louis. She hated the thought of being so far away from you, but she just couldn't get away from the strong conviction that St. Louis was where God wanted her. I think that is what impressed me the very most about Robyn — her desire to do God's will. In a graduation card she gave me last May, she said, "I hope God sees it in His divine plan that we work together. He always knows best and I will be happy with whatever his plan turns out to be." I am sure I will never understand while I'm on this earth why Robyn died. But thank God we

do not grieve as one who has no hope.
I look forward to the day when we will see
Robyn again! You must be so proud of her, and
you have every right to be.

I really want to stay in touch with
you. Just as you said, Mrs. Axman, that
keeping up with Robyn's friends reminds you
of Robyn - being around y'all and talking
with you reminds me of Robyn too.

I am praying for you.

Love,
Ramona

Dear Axmanns,

Robyn was one of my best friends a P.C. - she and I were in choir together, and lived on the same hall her senior year. She helped me decide my major, and encaraged me to participate in F.C.A. Robyn braght alot of happiness to me through her dawn-to-earth humor and commitment to the Lord. She is a true bright spot in my college career, and I regret that we didn't keep in touch afterward. I was never very worried when I found out she was sick because she was one of those people who seem "invinceable" — I guess those are the kind of people you miss the most.

Take care, you're in my prayers,

Ruth Woody

Comfort from
God's Word

A S I CLOSE my book, I want to leave you with some final thoughts and scriptures that have helped me through these impossible times in my life. I have written a lot of these verses and inspirational statements in the front of my Bible. I know at all times exactly where they are, and I read them over and over again and share them as the need surfaces in certain occasions.

I keep magazine articles, books, and sermons that encourage me and help me walk closer to God. The Sunday after we lost Robyn, we went to church and Dr. Alastair Walker preached a sermon that we felt was just for us. Here are notes from that message:

Scripture: 1 Peter 3:10–15; Psalm 34:12–16
David loved life!
1. Live in harmony.
2. Have compassion.
3. Love your brothers.
4. Be a blessing—an encourager.
5. Eyes of the Lord are on the righteous (v. 12) does not mean that he is going to protect you from pain. Paul and Silas prayed in prison in pain.

6. The night Jesus was betrayed, he took bread and gave thanks. Make him the Lord of your life.

Another sermon that helped me was "When Our Heart Breaks" by my pastor, Dr. Don Wilton. When our hearts are broken, we come back. Life is about surviving:

Scripture: Nehemiah 1:3–11
1. The walls and gates of Jerusalem (their protection) were broken down (v. 3).
2. Their leader heard. He wept (v. 4). If we don't stop and listen to God, we're in trouble.
3. He mourned. He had to die to self.
4. He fasted.
5. He prayed—sense of seriousness and to pour out grace, sense of humility.
6. He made three confessions:
   • Corporate confession (the people of Israel)
   • Personal confession
   • Generalized confession—"my father's house." In humility he presented his people. He exemplified a great sense of expectation (v. 11)—"Lord, let your ear be attentive TODAY!!!"

Another sermon that spoke to my need was called "When Your Faith Is Tested":

Scripture: Genesis 22
Ten Steps Related to Your Testing
1. Contact made (v. 1). God came to Abraham. He does this through his Word and through circumstances and through people.
2. Response heard (v. 1). "Here I am, Lord."
3. Instructions given (v. 2). Does God always give us specific instructions? No. He has a book of instructions.
4. Details followed (v. 3). Abraham followed in detail.

5. Questions asked. Questions asked are part of the journey of faith. There is nothing wrong with asking questions.

6. Faith taught. "God will provide the sacrifice, my son." Isaac was Abraham's only son, and Abraham was to be the father of many nations, and he was up in years. So he had a lot of questions for God.

7. Actions engaged (vv. 8–9).

8. Provision made (v. 11).

9. Awards given (v. 15).

10. Blessings received.

Scriptures I have listed in my Bible that have strengthened me along the way:

1 Peter 1:3–9

Colossians 3:23–24

1 John 3:1–10

Romans 15:13

Hebrews 11:1

Hebrews 10:23

Hebrews 11:6

Luke 11:32

Psalm 16:8–11

Ephesians 1:17–18

1 Peter 1:3–13

Psalm 27

1 Thessalonians 5:16–24

Psalm 91:2

Proverbs 3:5–6

Revelation 3:10

Romans 8:26–27

1 Corinthians 15:51–52

1 Thessalonians 2:16–17

Psalm 49:15

Philippians 4:19

Romans 8:38

Hebrews 4:16

1 Corinthians 2:9

Psalm 121

Exodus 17:7

Jeremiah 29:11

Jeremiah 17:7

Romans 7:24–25

John 5:28–30

John 4:14

Proverbs 17:22

1 Peter 1:3–7

Psalm 27:1–5

Psalm 73:26

1 Corinthians 15

Isaiah 44:33

Romans 8:9–11

Isaiah 54:10   Genesis 22:14
Ephesians 3:19–20   Luke 1:37
Exodus 20:1–3

Some important quotes have helped me, and I have jotted them down in the front of my Bible:

There is no pain as sharp as an uninterrupted pain, no tragedy as heavy as one without meaning. Paul's theology of the Cross provided all the meaning necessary to answer this and every painful situation.

No one can explain the tragedies just as no one can explain the miracles.

God will never let you down, nor will He let you off.—Dr. James Dobson

God will not reject a broken heart or a broken spirit. By His stripes we are healed.

God doesn't make mistakes.

When we do what we can, God will do what we can't.

What we get makes a living, but what we give and share makes a life.

Some of the things God asks us to do, do not make sense to us. (Example) Go and get a donkey for me to ride. We can't understand his ways at all times.—Avery Willis

God will not always deliver us from a crisis—he will deliver us through the crisis.

I am a pencil being used by God; in order to be successful, I must be used up!—Mother Teresa

All believers will be tested.

Nothing is impossible with God!

Our goal is not to be happy, but to glorify God!—Chuck Swindoll

Love is an action, not a word or an emotion.

Everything you experience will either make you bitter or make you better.

The greater the trial, the sweeter the victory.—George Muller (who lost a son and established orphanages).

ENCOURAGING OTHERS

I WAS ASKED TO write an article in my church newspaper. It expresses my thought on how God has helped me:

"Those who hope in the Lord will renew their strength. They will soar on wings like eagles; they will run and not grow weary, they will walk and not be faint"

—Isaiah 40:31

As the eagle soars under the baby eaglet, carefully watching to see that it doesn't fall, I can feel God's support as I try to wait on his direction in my life.

My husband, Bill, was my encourager and gave me strength when I was weak. We complimented each other and were so close. Our talents were different; what I was not talented in, he was, and what he was not talented in, I tried to make him think I knew all about it.

For example, when I was asked to finish out William's term as trustee at Anderson College, they put me on the finance committee where he had served. I informed them that, unlike my husband, finances were not my talent and they needed to place me on another committee. The only thing I knew about money was how to spend it.

William was such a stable Christian in every area of his life, and that was hard in the business world where he worked every day. He was committed to his church, his work, and his family. We did everything together, and I am so grateful for that love. Dr. Duke McCall expresses my feelings in a quote. One day someone said to him, "I'm sorry you lost your wife." Dr. McCall corrected his friend by saying, "I didn't lose my wife—I know where she is. I'm the one that's lost."

When we lost our daughter, Robyn, my husband and I became even closer as we were so distraught and confused about her loss. She was a beautiful Christian, had just graduated from Southern Seminary, and had already moved to St. Louis, where she was to work at an orphanage. She was such an inspiration and accomplished so much in her short life. I thank God for Robyn and a Christian son and daughter-in-law, and three beautiful grandchildren that bring such joy into my life.

Another scripture that has been an inspiration to me is 1 Peter 1:6–8, "You may have had to suffer grief in all kinds of trials. These have come so that your faith—of greater worth than gold, which perishes even though refined by fire—may be proved genuine and may result in praise, glory and honor when Jesus Christ is revealed."

Dr. David Jeremiah interprets it in a beautiful way. "When God permits his children to go through the furnace, he keeps his eye on the clock and his hand on the thermostat. His loving heart knows how much and how long."

The fire that chars the undergrowth around the tree strengthens the California Redwood tree, and as a result the tree reaches toward the sky for more light. It is able to expand and grow upward toward the light. Dr. Jeremiah also says if you are without chastening, then you are illegitimate and not sons. Sometimes my grief causes me to doubt. Doubt makes mountains that faith removes. My faith needs to be strengthened.

Like the new growth on the tree that reaches toward the light, my faith is reaching toward God to receive more light. God says, "Stay where you are and I'll be there with you." God has put his wings of strength under me, like the eaglet, to keep me going. The weaker I am, the stronger his grace is revealed. When this little light of mine becomes dimmer, his great floodlight shines all the more brightly. Some of the things I've learned in the darkest hour are things I should share in the light.

Robyn Axmann
Scholarships

AFTER WE LOST Robyn, we wanted to give back to the learning institutions she had attended and help some needy young persons complete their education, so we started scholarships everywhere Robyn had gone to school:

Robyn Axmann Scholarship at Anderson University in Anderson, Indiana

Robyn Axmann Scholarship at Presbyterian College in Clinton, South Carolina

Robyn Axmann Scholarship at Southern Seminary in Louisville, Kentucky

I also started a track scholarship in my husband's name:

William Axmann Scholarship at Furman University in Greenville, South Carolina

The thank-you notes I have received from the students who receive aid from the scholarships have been such a blessing to me. Praise God for these blessings.

SHE WON THE RACE

Robyn's Resume

MARTHA ROBYN AXMANN
Southern Baptist Theological Seminary
2825 Lexington Road
Box 1349
Louisville, Kentucky 40280
(502) 897-4376

PERSONAL

Age: 25, 2-1-65

Permanent Address: Parents; Mr. and Mrs William R. Axmann
308 Woodgrove Trace
Spartanburg, S.C. 29301
(803) 574-8579

EDUCATION

MASTERS OF SOCIAL WORK: Emphasis in Families, Individuals and Groups.
Southern Baptist Theological Seminary, Louisville Kentucky.
August 1987 - July 1990.

BACHELOR OF SCIENCE IN SOCIOLOGY: Minor in Christian Education.
Clinton Presbyterian College; Clinton, South Carolina.
August 1985 - May 1987.

ASSOCIATE OF ARTS IN SOCIOLOGY.
Anderson College, Anderson, South Carolina.
August 1984 - May 1985.

HONORS AND ACTIVITIES

OUTSTANDING SENIOR IN SOCIOLOGY; Presbyterian College, 1987.

RELIGION AND SPANISH SCHOLARSHIP; Anderson College, 1983.

DENMARK SOCIETY, Anderson College, 1985.

WHO'S WHO AMONG STUDENTS IN AMERICAN COLLEGES AND UNIVERSITIES;
Anderson College,1985.

FELLOWSHIP OF CHRISTIAN ATHLETES (SECRETARY);
Presbyterian College, 1987.

PRESBYTERIAN COLLEGE CHOIR; 1986-1987.

CAMPUS MINISTRIES, (PRESIDENT); Anderson College, 1985.

ANDERSON COLLEGE FRESHMAN AND SOPHMORE SENATE; 1983-85.

SELECTED BERMUDA MISSION TRIP; Anderson College, 1984.

HOBBIES AND INTERESTS

Jogging, Music, Basketball, and Tennis.

Robyn Axmann Scholarships

SOCIAL WORKER AND FAMILY COUNSLOR; Spring Meadows Children's Home, Middletown, Kentucky. August 1989 - Present.
    I was responsible for individual and group counseling with families. I developed and taught training seminars for campus Child Care Staff.

SOCIAL WORKER; Department of Social Services, Louisville, Kentucky. August 1988 - May 1989.
    I co-led training groups for perspective foster-care and adoptive parents. Conducted relative and independent adoptions which involved home assesments. Wrote court reports of completed adoptive research.

MINISTER OF YOUTH; Highland Park First Baptist Church, Louisville, Kentucky. June 1988-July 1990.
    Counseled with youth and their families, while providing appropriate training. Organized and led weekly Bible studies, fellowships, and other activities for the youth. Organized fund raisers for major events and trips. Coordinated events with area churches, along with other activities such as out of state trips.

CAMP COUNSELOR; Saddlerock Camp for Girls, Mentone, Alabama. Summer 1987.
    Music Teacher and Physical Education Leader; Director of Counselor Chorus, cabin counselor for ages 8-10.

RESIDENT ASSISTANT; Presbyterian College, Clinton, South Carolina, August 1986 - May 1987.
    Assisted Office of Student Affairs in providing leadership and advisement to students in the residence hall; supported and implemented policies and regulations of the college.

YOUTH WORKER; Central Presbyterian Church, Anderson, South Carolina. Summer, 1986.
    Responsible for planning Bible Studies, field trips, and other activities for pre-school age to college age groups. Gained experience in working with many different age groups.

YOUTH DIRECTOR; Riverstreet Baptist Church, Anderson, South Carolina. Summer, 1985.
    Planned activities for children and youth, led Bible studies, and planned fellowships for both age groups.

INSTRUCTOR; Children's Learning Center, Anderson, South Carolina. Summer, 1985.
    Taught arts and crafts, and planned and organized recreation and field trips.

STUDENT ASSISTANT; Dr. Samuel Arguez, Anderson College, Anderson, South Carolina. 1983-1985.

YOUTH COUNSELOR; Y.M.C.A. Anderson, South Carolina. 1983.

References

Dr. Diana Garland
Professor: Southern Baptist Theological Seminary

Sanford Kidd
Campus Minister: Anderson College

Ann Santora
Counselor: Spring Meadows Children's Home

William McMican
Family Counselor Supervisor—Kentucky State Social Worker

SHE WON THE RACE

Robyn with Jonathan